Dealing with the Therapist's Vulnerability to Depression

COMMENTARY

"The art of healing has often exacted a high price from psychiatrists and psychotherapists. Sheldon Heath devotes this book to the depression induced in the therapist. This usually occurs through the process of projective identification, a ubiquitous mechanism in all human relations, pathological and otherwise. Depression of the therapist might take the form of dysphoria, guilt, shame, helplessness, hopelessness, or even somatization. Worse still, the therapist might experience manic-like denial, contempt, or triumph, and hence resort to heroic measures, unnecessary interventions, and/or self-disclosures. The possibility that these symptoms and actions by caregivers might reflect the patient's own psychodynamics might be easily missed. The result could be a therapeutic impasse or rupture in the working relationship at the expense of the well-being of the client and the therapist. Dr. Heath—from his experience in the Tavistock and as a consultant to industry—goes further to alert the mental health worker of the possible malevolent influences that groups, for example, peers, administrators, case conferences, organizations, culture, and society, might exert on him or her. Finally, he advocates awareness by the therapist of the characterological tendency toward masochism inherent in choosing a helping profession in order to avert a sadomasochistic interaction with the help-rejecting patient/client."

—H. F. A. Azim, M.D.

"This book is a brilliant exploration of the depression that can afflict both therapist and patient. Sheldon Heath's ideas are fresh and thought-provoking, as he dares to investigate the therapist's depression and its role in the transference–countertransference relationship."

—Vamik D. Volkan, M.D.

"Sheldon Heath has provided a complete approach to the varieties of depressive experiences encountered in the mental health professions. He lays down a cogent, balanced object relations model of the intrapsychic origins of depression and its interpersonal dynamics. Next he describes the social elaboration of its phenomenology in individual therapy, supervision, inpatient wards, and other institutional groups. His readable style and intergrated overview of the subject make his book an essential guide for beginning therapists, who need the perspective and model for processing their own reactions. More experienced clinicians will learn from his sophisticated exposition of group and institutional reactions to their depressive anxieties and from the rich bibliography appended. Heath's book is clearly informative, inspiringly organized, and empowering."

—Ian Graham, M.D.

Dealing with the Therapist's Vulnerability to Depression

SHELDON HEATH, M.D.

JASON ARONSON
NORTHVALE, NEW JERSEY
LONDON

Library of Congress Cataloging-in-Publication Data

Heath, Sheldon.
   Dealing with the therapist's vulnerability to depression / Sheldon
Heath.
      p.   cm.
   Includes bibliographical references and index.
   ISBN 0-87668-612-9
   1. Psychotherapists—Mental health.   2. Depression, Mental.
3. Psychotherapist and patient.   I. Title.
   [DNLM: 1. Depression.   2. Professional-Patient Relations.
3. Psychotherapy.   WM 62 H438d]
RC451.4.P79H43   1991
616.85′27′0088616—dc20
DNLM/DLC
for Library of Congress   90-15591

Manufactured in the United States of America. Jason Aronson Inc. offers books and cassettes. For information and catalog write to Jason Aronson Inc., 230 Livingston Street, Northvale, New Jersey 07647.

To Iris Crossland Heath

Contents

Acknowledgment

My deepest appreciation goes to my colleague, Dr. Vamik Volkan, for his inspiration and encouragement.

It would be impossible not to mention the great influence of my earlier teachers and mentors at the Tavistock Clinic, London, England, who acquainted me with object relations theories and psychodynamic group theories in detail. I am especially grateful to the late Dr. Pierre Turquet for his invaluable discussions of the large group, the psychodynamics of which we discussed together as applying to institutes and associations.

Finally, I would like to thank my wife, Iris Heath, for her extensive editing of a dictated typescript into proper English. The dedication of this book to her is but a small reward.

1

Introduction

The working life of every therapist can be affected in varying degrees by a patient in reactive or endogenous depression or by depressive-like symptoms such as of futility, shame, or guilt. While therapists are rendered vulnerable by failures in therapy and in their personal lives, they are constantly affected by the transmission of affects and fantasies from their patients in all forms of therapy.

Therapists' vulnerability can be minimized by the strengthening of their internal psychological boundaries. They can then remain open to patients' projections without being overwhelmed by them. Furthermore, therapists' awareness of their vulnerability and of how the patient influences them can be extremely valuable in diagnosing what is disturbing the patient, and can be of major use in the formulation of effective interpretations. Thus, therapists' vulnerability to various forms of depression and depressive-like conditions not only is a natural occurrence in therapy but one that can be utilized, controlled, and reversed.

Small and large group psychodynamics affects the work life of patients, which in turn affects therapists and then institutions; and *their* psychodynamics affects both patient and therapists in powerful ways. The case conference and the clinic are examples of such groups. Cultural and language differences also may distort the therapeutic situation.

There seems to be considerable interest in the psychological difficulties of mental health professionals, in the problems of their children, and in the functioning or malfunctioning of their institutions (for example, Malcolm 1985). A current widely held belief is that many therapists are "wounded healers" (Maeder 1989). Whether or not the supposition is correct, it gives rise to more interesting questions. Do the mental health professions attract those with psychological problems, those, for example, who are trying to help themselves through their treatment of clients or patients? Are therapists, healthy or impaired, made more vulnerable by their professional work? If they are made vulnerable by their work, how do they protect themselves and how may they be helped to function better?

Prevalence studies in various populations sampled around the world suggest that nearly 20 percent of the population suffers from depressive symptoms (Persad 1989). Presumably, then, if a random sample were taken, a similar percentage of therapists would be suffering from the same symptomatology at any given time. The suggestion is, however, that more in the therapists' sample than in that of the general population have psychological problems. It is easy to say that the mental health field attracts those who are already casualties themselves, but it is necessary to look at the possibility that the stresses of practice affect practitioners in the field in major ways. A major stress on the therapist is dealing with depressed patients. Another is that depression is reactive to the stress of both effective and unsuccessful therapeutic work. The following chapters will consider depression *of* and *in* therapists, its cause, and its effects.

PROBLEMS IN DIAGNOSIS

Depressive symptoms in patients (and, of course, in therapists) cover a wide range of diagnostic categories, and the classification of depressive disorders is complex and sometimes arbitrary. Kendall (1976) reviews the then contemporary confusion and complains of the innumerable classification schemes. The American Psychiatric Association has attempted to address this complexity and confusion by providing so-called operational definitions of various types of depression. *Operational definitions* is a term that *sounds* more objective than the earlier *descriptive diagnoses*. Farmer and Mc-Guffin (1989), in their review of the classifications, assert that unipolar/bipolar depression has, indeed, been subtyped effectively. From their background of genetics research, however, they point out that "classification often reflects a whim or fashion or pressure of political persuasion. Inevitably . . . in recognizing this, we must also recognize that our classifications remain but working hypotheses" (pp. 441–442). They also point out that the hierarchy so necessary for clinical use seems to be disappearing under multiple diagnostic or multifactoral classifications. Even many patients previously diagnosed as having other "illnesses," such as schizophrenia, may be reclassified under affective disorder, including depression. In any event, although there is the useful clinical differentiation of reactive depression from endogenous depression, essentially the criteria of the *Diagnostic and Statistical Manual of the American Psychiatric Association III-Revised (DSM-III-R)* are intentionally descriptive ones rather than psychodynamic diagnoses. Phillips and colleagues (1990) comment on the change of depressive neurosis to dysthymia on axis I from *DSM-II* to *DSM-III* and argue the case for an axis II depressive personality disorder.

People, however, become depressed for a variety of reasons. Some feel depression due to guilt; some experience a sense of futility; some suffer blows to the narcissistic sense of self, masochistic self-doubt, and so on. These different depressions affect different therapists in different ways. Some types of reactive depression, for example, have the function of an appeal. Many therapists respond to this and are drawn into the patient's treatment. Some depressions, on the other hand, so manifestly affect the fundamental being of the therapist that he or she will withdraw from the patient or use some other coping mechanism. Few therapists deal well with massive regression, which may be one form of severe depression. Nor do they deal well with what Guntrip (1961, 1968) describes as the schizoid sense of futility. This is a fundamental inability to dialogue with an external object (which represents an internal object) in the form of relating to another person. In my view, it is a fault not only in schizoid personalities but in many patients who feel depressed. It is an inability shared by some who become psychotherapists. For many, psychotherapy is a tempting profession. Within the privacy of the consulting room, there is an opportunity to have an apparent dialogue with another without revealing oneself. In self psychology terms, the patient becomes a self-object for the therapist, mirroring his or her need to provide stability internally and enhance the self. Many patients, however, experience this sense of futility, and inability to relate to others, in such a confusing way that the experience is similar to a severe depression. Therapists tend to back away from the psychological chasm they see opening before them in these patients. Similarly, the therapist's reaction is commonly one of withdrawal when dealing with a patient who shows masochistic self-depreciating or a severe endogenous depression. As a personal coping mechanism, the therapist may reach hastily for his or her prescription pad to prescribe an antidepressant for the patient.

THERAPISTS AND COPING

The current psychosocial/biological approach to treatment swings heavily, in my view, to the biological side. This also may militate against looking for the psychological or social contributors to the patients' states. Studies indicate, however, that most of us will become depressed, to a major or minor degree, at some point in our lives. If the current tendency to prescribe antidepressant drugs to everyone who is depressed and has a personal or family history of depression persists, then soon there will be very few people left who do not qualify to be treated in this way, since most of us will have had a familial connection, at least, with someone who has been depressed.

Different therapists, as a result of their own personality development in childhood, are vulnerable to different degrees to the various depressive symptomatologies. Some therapists willingly treat reactive depression, the simple model of a patient who has lost his or her love object and has internalized the anger over such a real or imagined loss of the ambivalently loved object, since this is a common experience of all of us. Some therapists rehabilitate those with narcissistic problems as a way of healing their own bruised narcissism. Fortunately, as a result of the positive aspects of their childhood development in overcoming their depressions or their neurotic difficulties, many therapists have a "good fit" with their patients. They find the treatment of some depressive states very easy.

Less fortunate are those who face, consciously or unconsciously, the rupture of personal psychological boundaries between their patients and themselves. The maintenance of a personal boundary between patient and therapist means that the latter is attuned to his or her patient or client, listening with empathy but with the sense, nevertheless, that they are two distinct persons, not one psychological merger. Boundaries, however, are not barriers, and the transference and countertransference are reciprocal.

THE THERAPIST AS A DIAGNOSTIC INSTRUMENT

There are many opinions about the handling of the countertransference or counterreaction of the patient. My view extends the Kleinian one, in which the therapist uses the perceptions aroused in him- or herself as the patient is talking (or even *not* talking) as aids to interpretation. Bion (1962) originated the concept of "the container and the contained." The baby projects into the mother various unformed psychological elements that are "processed" by the mother, in an unconscious way, and returned. In that sense, the mother acts as a container for the baby's projective identifications. The baby identifies with the mother, so that he or she, likewise, develops an internal "container." Similarly, the therapist also has a psychic container that receives the patient's conscious or unconscious projections. Thus, the therapist may have "put into" him or her by the patient the patient's projective identifications, which, in turn, affect the therapist. The therapist receives the verbal and nonverbal communications from the patient and internalizes them into his or her ego and responds to them. If the patient is depressed, the therapist may have depression "put" or projected into him and thereby become depressed.

The recognition of this is a diagnostic tool, particularly of hidden or masked depressions. By identifying within him- or herself the depressed feelings, fantasies (conscious), and phantasies (unconscious), which have been put into him or her by the patient, the therapist can apprehend what is going on in the internal world of the patient or client and can use this understanding to formulate interpretations. I find useful the Kleinian differentiation of "fantasies," which are conscious, and "phantasies," which are unconscious.

OVERLOAD

The ego can be overwhelmed by the depressive fantasies (conscious) and phantasies (unconscious), as well as by the feelings put into the therapist. Even the conflict-free sphere of the ego, involving thinking, reflecting, evaluating, and synthesizing ideas, as described by Hartmann, Kriss, and Lowenstein (1946) can be infiltrated and invaded by depressive symptoms from other parts of the ego, sometimes without the therapist at first being aware. The therapist feels, in colloquial terms, overstressed, distressed, overloaded. The reestablishment of internal boundaries within the therapist's ego will relieve this and allow the therapist to be less vulnerable to the depressions experienced in the patient.

BACKGROUND FACTORS

Patients may be depressed by life situations; so therapists may be. Neither patients nor therapists operate in a vacuum. We are all members of groups and move from one group to another, from family to work unit, to committees and the like. Not only do we interact with one another as individuals, we are affected by the dynamics of the groups, the organizations, and the society of which we are a part. The resident in psychiatry responsible for the psychotically depressed patient is affected by the patient and by his or her supervisors, col-

leagues, and the nursing team. The patient is affected by the
resident and the nursing team. The nurse is affected by the
patient, the resident, and the group. The psychodynamics of
groups is a neglected area of psychotherapy and psychoanalysis. Since everyday groups and culture "implode" upon both
patient and therapist in health care delivery systems, as in all
organizations, understanding their psychodynamics is of very
great importance. Indeed, psychiatric diagnoses of patients
are often made in committee, by committees that are subject to
the psychodynamics of small groups. Often these are not
functioning groups. This calls into question the essence of
psychiatric and psychological diagnosis by case conference.

We are affected, too, *as therapists,* by major cultural factors
in our rapidly changing world. Patients from different cultures affect the professional's boundary maintenance in different ways. In a multicultural society, kinship may lead to
overidentification with a patient. On the other hand, when
treating a patient from a different culture, the therapist may
maintain unintentionally intense boundaries in certain areas.
Factors from the patient's "language," both verbal and nonverbal, affect the therapist. Even those who are doing research
and surveys of depression may be confused by the research
subjects they encounter in the interviews. Indeed, even apparently proven gender difference—that women either experience or have a tendency to report depressive episodes more
than men—is open to serious question (McGuffin and Katz
1989). These authors remind us that the "liability to develop
depressive illness and propensity to experience (or report)
unpleasant events are different manifestations of the same
familial diathesis" (p. 303).

Awareness, then, that there is interaction between subject
and researcher, student and counselor, patient and analyst,
psychiatrist, psychologist, family practitioner, social worker,
resident, and nurse is important. Insight into the nature of a
patient's depression and what he or she does with that depres-

sion brings understanding of the boundary between the healer and the to-be-healed. Boundaries allow a psychological distance between the therapist and the patient without loss of empathy. They prevent the therapist from being overwhelmed by the patient's depressive symptomatology and allow the therapist to use his or her own fantasies and feelings about the patient, which are reactions to the patient or the patient's projections, for the formulation of interpretations. The number of psychiatrists, psychologists, residents, trainees, nurses, social workers, counselors, and family practitioners who care for depressed patients and clients in many countries is very large. We can only conclude, therefore, that the number of health care professionals who are vulnerable to depression is large. We see evidence of this in ourselves and our colleagues in our everyday professional lives. It is an important phenomenon that should be examined: a therapist's vulnerability to depression is profound.

2

Depressive Symptomatologies

In revisions of the diagnostic criteria for depressions—*DSM-III-R*, for example—current positions about criteria are intentionally descriptive (and labeled "operational definitions") rather than psychodynamic diagnoses. Mood disorders are diagnosed from mild to psychotic and contain subcodings as to the state of remission. Depressive disorders are classified as major depression (single episode or recurrent) or dysthymic disorder (depressive neurosis). A useful clinical variation of this classification (Persad 1989) can be as follows:

> chronic depression
> dysthymic disorder or depressive neurosis
> atypical depression
> psychotic or endogenous depression
> bipolar depression.

Whereas this form of diagnosis is believed to have many advantages, for our purpose it is necessary to look at the psychological interrelationship between the patient or client and the therapist; from this point of view, a descriptive diagnosis is of limited use. It is questionable if by simply renaming descriptive criteria "operational definitions," the criteria are made more valid.

HOW COMMON IS DEPRESSION?

Depressive symptoms in varying degrees of severity are estimated to be present in 20 percent of the adult population in surveys around countries in the world. The rate is said to be even higher (up to 35 percent) when mild cases are included, and it is especially high in those who are visiting general practitioners or medical clinics (Persad 1989). Incidences of disguised depression may not be included in such prevalence surveys. Some practitioners suggest that if those patients presenting to a family practitioner with disguised depression are added to those with overt depression, the number may constitute 50 percent of his or her cases.

There are concerns that the rate of depression is increasing. Other studies (e.g., Bebbington et al., 1988) find that seven out of ten women and four out of ten men in a London suburb had a clinically significant depressive episode by the age of 65. So much depends on the definition of what constitutes a case of depression, however, that there are large variations in prevalence estimates (Eastwood and Kramer 1981). In a Swedish study of the incidence of depression in a small community (Rorsman et al. 1990), incidence being the liability to develop the illness, the cumulative probability of developing a first depression by 70 years of age was 27 percent in men and 45 percent in women.

Murphy (1990) reminds us of the wide range of reported prevalence of depression, from 17 percent to 50 percent of various populations (prevalence being the number ill at one period of time, whereas incidence is an enumeration of those who will experience a first episode over a defined period of time). She feels that prevalence studies underrepresent those who become afflicted and then recover after a short period. She reports a 1970 epidemiology study of the point prevalence of depression with or without anxiety (point prevalence being those with symptoms at a particular moment) in a longitudinal study of a county in Atlantic Canada and finds this to be 5.6 percent. Murphy also tables an overview of similar point prevalence studies of six other North American urban and rural communities, plus one in 1952 in the same Atlantic Canada county. The current point prevalence of major depression varies over a very narrow range (4–6 percent of an adult population).

Percentages of depression depend upon the sampling method, the degree of severity, and the diagnostic tools used. For clinical as opposed to epidemiological purposes, however, the prevalence rate over a year for all ranges of depression is more important than the point prevalence rate (the rate at the given moment) or the prevalence over a group of clinicians' professional lifetimes, if such could be sampled.

SPONTANEOUS CHANGES

Although it is easy to think of a biopsychosocial model for mental health problems—and the search for a genetic factor in depressions is important—nevertheless, in my view, the depressive symptomatologies as described are still obscured by descriptive pictures. Furthermore, depressions and the varying nature of depressions may have different effects, and thus produce different responses, in different diagnosticians. It is crucial, therefore, to look at the subtypes of depressions, not only in terms of psychobiosocial diagnoses but in terms of psychodynamic ones. It is useful, too, to consider the potential for interaction between the patient and the therapist.

Eysenck (1965) is critical of the value of psychotherapy because he concluded from a study that two-thirds of psychological disorders, including neurotic depressions, would remit spontaneously. In a study in which I participated, we looked at patients who had received only one consultation and a follow-up at the Tavistock Clinic, London, England. They did not continue treatment because of distance, lack of motivation, or extraneous factors. Our conclusions were that the symptomatology did, indeed, disappear in 63 percent of the forty-five patients who had a variety of diagnoses of a neurotic nature, whom we interviewed in follow-up. The crucial factor, however, in our view, was that underlying psychodynamics in thirty-four of these forty-five patients had not changed in any major way. Put simply, while they may have lost their symptoms for a time, these people were essentially the same. It may therefore be possible to say that psychoneurotic depressive disorders are time limited and have a tendency to recur, but relapses may occur not because of lack of treatment of the symptoms but because the underlying psychodynamics have not been dealt with. It is important, also, to understand the influence they may have upon the therapist and upon a researcher. Many of the patients in the above study might have benefited from interpretive psychotherapy to attempt to change the underlying psychopathology.

REACTIVE DEPRESSION

Forms of reactive depression can range from mild to severe in intensity, and it is tempting to treat them with psychotherapy of a directive kind, with social support and medication, or, in severe depressions, with more definitive methods, such as electroconvulsive therapy (ECT). The underlying etiology of reactive depression, which was shown by Freud, may, however, still be of use because it leads to therapy aiming at deeper change of predisposing personality factors.

Freud (1917) describes, in this critical paper, how the depression we now term *reactive depression* follows a real or phantasied loss of an external object, which is then introjected into the unconscious and identified with. Because this is an ambivalently loved object, the anger present is directed in an accusatory way toward the self, although, theoretically more correctly, toward an ambivalently loved and hated lost object representation within the self. Freud points out that a characteristic of the depressed patient, in contrast to the grieving patient, is that he or she does not see a light at the end of the tunnel.

> Christopher, a psychiatric resident, was jilted by Jill, his lover of a year because, ostensibly due to religious differences, he did not want to marry her. The precipitating factor, in retrospect, may have been his plan to continue his residency in another city, leaving Jill behind. He was distraught when she began to go out with other men and told him that she was doing so.
>
> Christopher found himself devastated, and on a descriptive basis, might have been termed moderately to severely depressed. He drank heavily to get himself to sleep, brooded about Jill constantly, and reproached himself for not having handled the affair better. He alternated between rage at the perfidy of women in general and at himself for his ineptitude in not being in control of the situation. When he moved to complete his residency training in another city, he felt some relief of his symptoms. A review of what had happened came out in his analysis. Some of his feelings about Jill were revealed in his venting anger upon the next woman in his life, Janice, who seemed to be very fond of him. He argued that he had to postpone marriage for the sake of his career. He also used his commitment to his personal analysis as an excuse not to become more involved with her.

It would have been easy to have put Christopher on an antidepressant and to have considered that his depressive symptoms would have resolved themselves spontaneously in a number of months. Indeed they did so, helped by his move to a nearby city where he no longer saw reminders of Jill. His depression had recurred, for example, whenever he heard music they had listened to together, or whenever he had had to drive past her house on his way to work.

RESCUE FANTASIES AND CONTEMPT

Patients like Christopher evoke powerful conscious fantasies and unconscious phantasies in mental health workers, who see themselves rescuing them. There are few of us who have not experienced a reactive depression of a similar nature. Few have not suffered loss from a social relationship or a love affair and not experienced a similar symptom pattern. The reactive depression for most therapists, therefore, has the function of an appeal. This appeal function has been described by Olinick (1980), who suggests "a powerful motivation . . . is the genetic effect of a rescue fantasy having to do with a depressive mother, the latter having induced such a rescue fantasy in her receptive child." In treating these patients who have experienced a loss, there is often recourse to the simple model of the reactive depression: the patient is depressed because he or she cannot direct his anger at the loss, at the external target (which reflects the internal object), and so redirects this anger toward the ambivalently loved internal object—thereby toward the self. There is then an attempt to have the patient or client review the angry feelings, which are often concealed, and to have them brought into the open in the session.

If there is a recurrence of the reactive depression, the therapist is moved to look at the sufferer's underlying character structure. He or she feels continued sympathy and empathy unless the depressions are recurrent and the underlying causes of the patient's need to be involved in repetitive disastrous relationships are unresolved. If the recurrent object relationship patterns are clearly defined to the patient with good results, the therapist's anxiety is diminished. The analysis of therapists themselves, however, often reveals contempt for those patients who cannot get sufficient insight or cannot work through their difficulties to an adequate degree.

As we know, contempt is a manic defense against an underlying depression (Segal 1973). It is a not uncommon defense in therapists. The therapist's feelings of contempt for a patient who gets into recurrent bad relationships arises from a sense of frustration within the psychotherapy or psychoanalysis. The therapist may belittle the patient to colleagues as a way of handling the depression that is evoked within him- or herself. This depression in the therapist has a number of components. The despondent patient may, as his or her depressions recur, project them into the therapist by the process of projective identification. The therapist may also react to the real or imagined failure of the treatment with feelings of inadequacy.

DEFENSES—DEFINITIONS

It is helpful to define some defenses against depression at this point.

Projection—unacceptable thoughts, impulses, or feelings are attributed to someone else.

Projective Identification—parts of the self are projected into an internal object within the internal world. This is seen in the external world as a projection into a part or whole of an external object. The self of the individual who projects is then, in part or in full, identified with the projected part of the object in the other person.

Manic Defenses (Segal 1973)—the defenses against the experience of depression, guilt, or loss. They are based upon omnipotence or omnipotent denial and are:

Triumph—denying the depressive feelings of valuing, caring for, and missing the lost object.

Control—compelling the object to be dependent while denying dependence upon the object.

Contempt—denying valuing the lost object, defending against the experience of loss and guilt. Contempt justifies further attacks upon the lost object.

RESOLUTION

Rescue fantasies are in themselves warning signs that the therapist may not be sufficiently detached from the patient. If they arise, it may be necessary for the therapist to explore the reasons for them in terms of his or her own life experiences. If the therapist feels contempt for the patient, or is tempted to ridicule or belittle him or her, either in the therapist's own mind or to colleagues in case conferences and the like, then self-scrutiny is required. Contempt for a patient is a symptom of a usually hidden depression within the therapist about their work together.

Christopher, the psychiatric resident, had a successful psychoanalytic result. He established another relationship with fewer of the depressive qualities concerned. He explored the relationship he had had with his mother and understood his need to take out his feelings upon his women friends. His ambivalence toward women came into his analysis. The analyst in turn was able to recognize his own initial rescue fantasies—he had been a resident himself and had experienced similar losses—which were replaced by slight disdain for a patient who could neither seem to come to grips with his problems nor overcome these recurring patterns. By self-analysis, the analyst was able to see the effect of his patient upon himself, and thus avoid being destabilized by him to even a minor degree. He was, therefore, able to provide effective help in the form of insight by interpretations.

PSYCHOTIC, ENDOGENOUS, AND BIPOLAR DEPRESSIONS

Psychotic depression, or what used to be called endogenous depression, and bipolar depression may very well have important biological (genetic and biochemical) factors in their etiology. Here there is no precipitating cause and the depression is worse in the morning, a symptom being early morning awakening. There may be vegetative symptoms and signs, loss of appetite, weight loss, and psychomotor retardation. Fatigue or loss of energy is a common complaint. There are often quite unrealistic feelings of worthlessness, sinfulness, and guilt. There may be recurrent thoughts of death or suicide and of the worthlessness of a life that for the patient has no interest or pleasure.

The intensely depressed mood of the endogenous depression is not easy for most therapists of any persuasion to deal with. Whereas the current method of treatment is the use of antidepressant drugs, the waiting period for these to take effect—two to six weeks—is an anxiety-provoking time for the psychiatrist who has written the prescription. The recommendation for major depressions when antidepressant drugs fail, as they do in 30 percent of cases, is currently to resort to ECT. It might, however, be useful to describe how in my own residency some years ago we were not permitted to use drugs. Patients such as these were treated on an inpatient basis by psychological methods, including a supportive nursing experience. My own anxiety about this was overcome by the realization that providing a supportive therapeutic "facilitating environment" (Winnicott 1965) was in itself useful. It must be remembered that Balint (1957) said, "The most important drug the doctor has is the doctor." The counterargument, from a biological point of view, is that we were simply providing supportive therapy for these severe depressions while the depression took a natural course. The treatment results with biological methods may be exactly the same. The argument for using drugs is that they shorten the natural course. This needs to be checked by comparison studies.

Depressed patients can be extremely depressing. Severe or major depressions evoke many responses in psychotherapists—feelings of hopelessness, anxiety about a possible suicide, and so forth—and they are a threat to one's personal sense of omnipotence. To allay one's own feelings when treating severe depressions, there is often a hasty reach for the prescription pad or the ordering of electroconvulsive therapy. The question is: For whose benefit is the drug prescription really, the psychiatrist's or the patient's?

Dr. R. was a very successful family practitioner in the community. He complained to one of my colleagues that he was extremely depressed and that he had no interest in his work and was barely able to function at it. A major symptom was his inability to fall asleep, in addition to which he would wake early in the morning and continue to brood about his life. He felt worthless. He was quite agitated. He was consumed by guilt about what he had done in his childhood to his mother, who was chronically depressed. She had blamed him for all her problems and said that living with him as a child was worse than being in the concentration camp. He thought about suicide, although how seriously he did so is not very clear. There was a family history of depression. Were there any precipitating factors? He was unmarried but was in process of establishing a good relationship with a woman he found very attractive. There were some difficulties at work in his hospital. One of the nurses was complaining about his irritable behavior as a surgical assistant in the operating room. My colleague placed him on a tricyclic antidepressant, and because the physician was appealing and a colleague, probably on the basis of sympathy, referred him for intensive psychotherapy, presumably in conjunction with the drugs.

My major therapeutic tactic with Dr. R. was to take him into a modified analysis on a three-times-a-week basis on the couch.

Some readers will react with surprise to this approach on the grounds that the use of the analytic couch fosters or favors regression and theoretically, therefore, should have made the patient worse. My own thinking was that I could provide a therapeutic holding and facilitating environment that would allow him to feel comfortable even in a regressed state, where he could review his feelings of guilt and worthlessness and link these historically with episodes from his early childhood, with his mother and, to a certain extent, with his father. His parents had blamed him for most of the unhappiness in the family, and the patient suffered from intense feelings of guilt.

Secondly, although my colleague had said that, because his mother and an uncle were also depressed, Dr. R. was obviously suffering from a major depression with biological, probably with hereditary, components and had referred him to me for therapy as an adjunct to the drug therapy, I nevertheless suggested to Dr. R. that he stop taking the antidepressant drug, which he seemed to be taking by his own decision mainly as a sleeping medication due to the drug's side effects. He felt relieved that at last someone in his life was listening to him in a different way, with an uncritical and nonjudgmental attitude. His self-depreciating component had to be dealt with. It was useful to him to have pointed out his continual need to think that every problem in the world, including those, rationally, far from his area of responsibility, were due to him. He was concerned about his insomnia. Since a side effect of the antidepressant drug was to make him sleepy, he continued to take one pill intermittently at night for a short period of time in his therapy, as a sleeping pill substitute. This combined with a large glass of whisky allowed him to get a good night's sleep and, thus, perform better at his job.

Over the next few weeks his depressed mood lifted considerably. He regained an interest in his work. The agitated aspects of his depression decreased and his energy level increased. He began to feel that he was a good doctor and, also, that it would be worthwhile developing his relationship with the woman in his life.

Critics might think that Dr. R. had been referred to me at a certain phase in a spontaneous remission of his major depression. I do not think so. I believe that providing him with a therapeutic environment, supporting him, and making interpretations to him about his superego guilt and its effects upon him, were extremely helpful.

Dr. R.'s delusions of worthlessness had made him believe he was the cause of difficulties with the nurses at the hospital. He saw that the problems were their problems, and began to think that the nurses might have picked on him because of their difficulties with others in the hospital. Further intensive exploration helped him see how his mother and, to a lesser extent, his father had induced guilt feelings in him. He was a natural carrier of guilt.

I believed that the antidepressant drug at this point was only serving as a sedative, which, with the alcohol, allowed him to have a good night's sleep. The sleep contributed to the reversal of the depressive process because by feeling refreshed, he gained feelings of self-control. I therefore delegated to him the responsibility for deciding whether or not to continue taking the drug. The fact that he was in control of his life again gave Dr. R. temendous self-confidence.

Dr. R. elected to continue taking the drug although, as a doctor, he agreed that it probably had only a placebo effect. He stopped taking it after two weeks. He continued in analysis, however.

Dr. R. ultimately married the woman who had entered his life. He has had no recurrence within six years of his apparent "major depression" to which the doctor who referred him thought he had a genetic predisposition.

CHRONIC DEPRESSION

This is characterized descriptively by remission and recurrence, and may persist over several years with varying degrees of severity. It is said to account for 10 to 15 percent of the depressed. How useful this classification is, again, questionable. As mentioned previously, Phillips and colleagues (1990) state the case for the existence of the depressive personality. Plainly chronic depression should be differentiated from bipolar disorder, and from the type of recurrent bipolar disorder whose depressive phases return over and over again without manic or mixed episodes.

My experience of dealing with people who are considered to have chronic depression is that often there have been one or more prior attempts to treat them with tricyclic or other forms of antidepressant. The resultant benefits have been temporary and possibly had a placebo effect.

Some chronic depressions and some of the atypical depressions are supposed to be responsive to environmental stimuli, hypersensitivity to rejection (real or imagined), and have reversed vegetative symptoms, overeating and oversleeping, for example. Some chronic depressions are often associated with other major psychiatric syndromes, such as schizophrenia. I suspect that some depressive patients are being put into the category because they have a symptomatology that is similar to depression but is not, in fact, the same. Fairbairn (1952) and Guntrip (1961, 1968) have described patients who do not suffer from a loss, real or imagined, of an external person or object (representing an internal object) and so do not fall into the category termed *reactive depression,* but may fall into the category subsumed under *chronic depression.* It is therefore possible that our current prevalence studies of depression may be somewhat skewed if patients with a recurrent or continuous sense of futility are included in the depressive categories.

THE SCHIZOID SENSE OF FUTILITY

The category of patients Fairbairn and Guntrip describe is one that is not uncommon in my clinical experience. They are people who are afraid of a close relationship because it is too dangerous. These patients explain, when asked, that they do not have a depression but a sense of futility, that they cannot relate to the world or the people in it, and that these symptoms are chronic. They have transitory relations with others but because of their inability to deal with such relationships, these are often ended, either by themselves or by their partners.

Guntrip (1968) asserts that underneath they have a fear of destroying the loved object or that the other may do the same to them. This Guntrip attributes to unconscious oral sadism. Many of the patients experience this. Others simply fear that the desired object is unobtainable, and therefore they do not even bother to try. They withdraw. They also fear absorption by the other person or object.

The characteristic of those who have a schizoid core is introversion, with detachment inwardly and away from external objects in the outer world. They often have a wealth and richness of inner fantasies. They are withdrawn and somewhat narcissistic. Their focus is primarily upon the self. They have an intense need for self-sufficiency, as external objects or people are meager, and they fear that external objects cannot be trusted. Sometimes they have a sense of superiority that overcompensates the need, or craving, for deep-seated dependence on people. Internally and unconsciously, therefore, they may have feelings of inferiority and weakness. Loss of affect is part of the picture. Loneliness is inescapable. There is a sense of some depersonalization, feelings of loss of identity and individuality, and a derealization of the outer world. The person with the sense of futility feels overwhelmed by the external world and regresses inwardly. The underlying motivation is fear. It is important to note that the underlying psychodynamic is not guilt, or related to rage, but is fear of a frightening outer world (Guntrip 1968).

While I do not have prevalence studies for the sense of futility, in my clinical experience, as I have said, it is common, and not only in those diagnosable as schizoid personalities. It is also often encountered in social situations, since many sufferers do not go into therapy, because a component they experience constantly is a sense of hopelessness about their state. If even a therapeutic experience and a therapist are regarded as related to objects that will let them down, that will only lead to a sense of futility and failure, why get involved?

In these cases there are, obviously, environmental factors that are similar to those involved in a milder form of depression, a chronic depression, or a dysthymic or a typical depression, but there are differences.

THE DIFFERENCES

Careful scrutiny of this type of patient reveals they are not suffering typical loss of a loved object, real or fantasied. There may be minor discontents if the patient has broken off a relationship, or if the other person has tired. There is, however, no experience of loss, since a person with a schizoid sense of futility is prepared for the failure of human relations. There is little loss of aggressive or sexual feelings but an attempt to suppress them. They may be projected onto others, leading to a withdrawal from these others.

A simple diagnostic tool is to *ask* the patient whether he or she feels depressed or feels futile. Many of my patients have been astonished by the question but more astonished by their own response. From their sense of their inner world they can perceive the difference quite clearly. They do not feel depressed or angry: they feel hopeless and unable to relate.

Karen, a 55-year-old divorced woman, was referred for treatment because she was obese, unable to comply with her antihypertensive medication, and had symptoms of a chronic depression. She was the ninth child in a family of ten and had been brought up by a mother who wished to be supportive but who simply did not have time for all of them. The father was a chronic gambler and was little involved in the family.

Karen needed to repeat her mother's experience and thereby, unconsciously, to be with her mother by having a large number of children with a husband who sounded very similar to her father. She enjoyed the experience of giving birth and the feeling that she was needed and could love a baby, though not a child. Babies, however, grow up and develop personalities of their own. Karen coped in a loving way as best she could and after her divorce, despite her financial situation, provided for them—her divorce settlement was not sufficient and times were often hard, but she was an intelligent woman and, as she remarked, a survivor. What is important is that she felt she could never trust people. She said that what she did for her children and grandchildren she did from a sense of duty: people were wrong to assume that she did these things out of generosity. She felt that life was hopeless. If she were at home she would watch television all day simply for something to do. She had a good job in a corporation and her employers were delighted to have her because she spent many hours of unpaid overtime there, producing quality work. She said that her workplace was the only real home she had ever had. She did not bother to apply for promotions because she saw no point in doing so. When friends invited her on holidays she went along; "but," she remarked, "they did not know that I was not really there with them."

I saw Karen once a week in therapy for several years. A nonjudgmental attitude about her overeating and her non-compliance about the antihypertensive medication gained me a certain amount of trust from her. Her sessions were filled with the sense of futility. She was, in fact, quite pleased on her first visit when I asked her my classic question: Was she depressed or did she have a sense of futility? She said that the latter described her feelings very aptly, and she was not depressed; she simply could not relate to people and had no interest in doing so; people were basically untrustworthy and one could not love them. She came to her sessions expecting little, but she began to feel that someone who could not possibly help to change her nevertheless understood her. She began to take her antihypertensive medication because she began to feel that, maybe, life might have some worth.

An interesting part of her therapeutic change was an indirect interest in myself through the work I did. She began to read psychological books on attachment theory and philosophical books on existentialism.

I reacted to this patient, initially, with a sense of hopelessness. I can assure the reader there was no appealing element in Karen's case. On the contrary, my own existential fantasies were stimulated by my sessions with her. Was she right? Was my life a facade? Did we really not love those around us? Was I doing my work as a therapist only for financial reward?

It came to me that these feelings, which were intense, were stirred up in me by the patient, and that she was probably projecting into me the very feelings that she had about herself. I reflected these back to her in her therapy, and we discussed them (she talked about her absolute honesty, for example, but gradually revealed her minor transgressions at work. She needed the self-perception that she was honest to reassure herself that she was probably like the rest of us, professing honesty but covering up our dishonesty—her view, not mine). One of her themes was the ineffectiveness of trying to change the past. My comment that one's attitude toward the past was changeable had some effect. Still she continued to arouse in me intense feelings of doubt about why I was doing this work. Was it really that within myself I, also, had a schizoid core? Was there any point in psychoanalysis or psychotherapy when both were under attack in the medical and psychiatric world in which I practice?

It was helpful to me to realize that these doubts had been evoked in me by the patient, and that unpleasant as they were, they might in fact be a healthy response to her, and might be a useful part of the ongoing process of self-scrutiny that all therapists are supposed to undergo.

DISRUPTIONS IN THE SELF

Kohut and his followers have developed the theories of self psychology that have had a major influence on psychotherapy, particularly in North America. Adherents of these theories propound a totally different development of the self. They point out that ruptures in the development of the narcissistic sense of self may lead to an affect that has a symptomatology very similar to depression. Self psychologists suggest, however, that this affect is not principally depression, which is based on rejection, but is a sense of shame.

Patty, 32 years old and recently separated from her husband of eight years, came for treatment because she complained of being depressed. She suffered repeated outbursts of crying, was unable to sleep at night, and was unable to function in work she had previously done well. History-taking revealed that she had suffered minor episodes of these symptoms since the death of her mother five years before.

Patty had grown up in a household dominated by the rigid standards of a repressive maternal grandmother. Her mother, too, was intolerant of any display of weakness. Nor did she give Patty adequate "mirroring" in her childhood. Any achievement, for example, was greeted with a caution against "showing off," against displaying the "sin of pride." On these occasions, Patty would run crying to her room, ashamed that she was unable ever to live up to her mother's standards. These feelings persisted into adulthood. As a grown woman, reading a novel, she would compare herself unfavorably with the heroine of the book and would experience the emotional instability she had experienced as a child.

Patty's father was rarely in the house as she was growing up. He was an alcoholic, and was a source of shame and embarrassment to Patty and her sisters, who, it transpired, also suffered from similar crying fits. Patty cried about her father in the sessions. Even memories of him produced a temporary rupture of her narcissistic defenses.

Patty's husband had dominated her, and had frequently berated her about her various character traits.

Patty was suffering not from depression but from shame; shame that she could not live up to her husband's standards, or those of her mother.

The sense of shame and the sense of guilt are hard to distinguish from depression, and may lead to confusion among diagnoses. This is true even in classifications such as *DSM-III-R* classification systems.

Ruptures of the sense of self in the patient within therapy or in a consultation can upset the therapist. Therapeutic work in itself, at times, can be very threatening. Passive disruptions in ego-functioning are often seen in therapy, and may lead to instability in the therapist and affect his or her response to the patient. The therapist's narcissism may make him or her wish for uninterrupted progress in the treatment. The patient's temporary setbacks threaten this narcissism. Since these disruptions occur in all therapies, therapists suffer repeated minor or major disruptions of the sense of self. The therapist may react to the patient (by giving advice, for example, or by leaping in with an intervention) primarily to protect him- or herself rather than to restore the patient. This, in turn, affects the counterreaction or countertransference.

MASOCHISTIC SELF-DEPRECIATION

The etiology of masochism is complex, and space does not permit us to deal with it except in terms of symptomatology.

Constant repetitive masochistic depreciation may be a symptom of depression or part of a masochistic character disorder. The effect upon the therapist can be intense, sometimes devastating.

There is little a masochist can do that is not a form of self-depreciation. Every success in therapy, as in life, is but a preamble to a further downer. For a therapist the work is difficult, but gradually the masochistic patient can see the repeated pattern and make psychological gains. This takes time. Long-term therapy, including psychoanalysis, is required. Usually, eventually, the masochism is ameliorated. The patient can catch him- or herself dealing with a situation in a particular way and can then stop. One problem is the toll upon the therapist before that point is reached.

At first the therapist tolerates the effects of the patient's masochism as a part and parcel of everyday work. But after a while the repeated failure within the therapeutic situation, and the listening to the seemingly interminable self-depreciation and to the constant viewing of the world in a self-centered or narcissistic way is profoundly depressing to most therapists. If the patient has mildly depressive symptoms, as a result of the masochistic self-depreciation or self-scrutiny, there may be apparent justification for shifting the diagnosis into one of the depressive categories and for prescribing, therefore, an anti-depressant drug. The temptation to reach for the prescription pad is very great.

The second reaction to masochistic patients is one of contempt. This, again, is a hidden form of depression in the therapist. It allows a psychological distancing of the therapist from the patient. After contempt, masochistic patients evoke hostile reactions in their therapists. These may take the form of "helpful suggestions," sarcasm, or open hostility.

These responses by the therapist are symptoms of a mild reactive depression induced by a difficult patient. Even a mild reaction, such as impatience with the patient and "hurrying" him or her, is a result of the therapist's trying to deal with his or her own feelings. The primary treatment for the therapist is self-analysis and self-scrutiny; for the patient it is protective understanding and interpretation. It is interesting how one can change from feeling contempt for a patient, from disliking a patient, even hating a patient, into understanding and supporting him or her when one sees the effect the patient has upon oneself.

Rita was the fifth daughter in a family of seven. The younger two children were boys. Rita's mother had always impressed upon her daughters the importance of "catching a man," which for her was a woman's only function. The sisters and the mother were, apparently, very resentful of Rita because almost all of her life, on the rare occasions when he had been present, her father had singled her out. He was very taken by her intelligence and girlish charm. Rita's mother, however, brought up all her daughters to think that they were useless.

Rita was brought up to be guilt prone. She constantly depreciated herself. She took guilt upon herself. Because she had internalized the mother as a harsh superego object, the mother's criticism became internal and identified with. It became Rita's criticism of herself, and was certainly as harsh as was her mother's, possibly even more so. Analytic work revealed that from an early age Rita had projected her own violence into her mother. The mother, therefore, in phantasy was then more violent toward her. Rita's superego became even harsher than the real mother and the criticisms, in turn, became harsher.

Rita acted out the family script assigned to her. She was quite carefree in university and had to drop out. She drifted from job to job. Because of her high intelligence she was given a trial as a manager in one organization, but because of her self-depreciation, she was never able to present herself as an adequate person and was let go. Subsequently, job search after job search was unsuccessful, and she felt more and more hopeless about herself.

Her effect upon her analyst was sometimes quite profound. He became impatient with her in her job searches, and was drawn into making suggestions. Her masochistic depreciation to her colleagues when she was working, and to her bosses, irritated him and he began to wonder if he had been referred a hopeless case. He directed his anger toward the colleague who had shunted this patient onto him. At times he felt drawn into her self-derogation and wondered if she were not the awful person she described. Here again we see the boundaries between patient and therapist being broken, and the therapist being drawn in to play the role of the critical mother-object. Fortunately, the therapist's recognition of this allowed him to back away into a more therapeutic stance. He lost his impatience with her and his identification with the critical employers, who were at times merely objects of her own projective system of the critical mother. Of course, in reality some employers were critical, but Rita evoked and provoked much of the criticism herself.

In the course of time and treatment she gained self-awareness. She became successful in a managerial position and took university courses in her spare time to complete her degree.

Here we see another apparent depression that proves to be something else, and that requires a form of treatment different from an antidepressant.

To sum up: all therapists are hated by patients at times, in the transference. This hatred threatens the therapist's sense of self by inflicting narcissistic wounds that lead to feelings of shame and worthlessness. Similarly, no therapists are exempt from the massive depressive affects of various forms that patients project into them. Therapists, therefore, are prime targets of intense feelings aroused in them by patients, directly as a reaction to the patient and also—because the therapist is attentive and receptive to his or her patient—by projective identification of depressed patients' feelings. The work of therapy itself renders therapists vulnerable, but as I hope to show throughout this book, this very vulnerability may be to the therapist's advantage, and not to his or her disadvantage.

3

The Transference–Countertransference Paradigm

At the outset, I should point out that I take an extended view of the transference–countertransference. An extended set of models is necessary to explain the effects that patients and clients have upon their therapists and especially to explain how the depressive symptoms of patients make their therapists vulnerable. Many of my conclusions come from previous contributors and it may be helpful to look at some of these.

To enter into any discussion of transference, countertransference, projective identification, transference interpretation, empathy, and so on is to enter a series of multiple labyrinths since there are ongoing debates about each one of these concepts. Laplanche and Pontalis in *The Language of Psychoanalysis* (1973) feel that it is difficult to provide a definition of transference since, for many authors, the concept has taken on "a broad extension, even coming to connote all the phenomena which constitute the patient's relationship with the analyst." Therefore "each analyst's particular views in the

35

treatment . . . are a subjective dynamics, tactics, scope, etc."
Even then "the question of transference is beset by a whole
series of difficulties which have been the subject of debate in
classical psychoanalysis" (p. 456). Cooper (1987) suggests
that we may never clearly understand what any two people
mean when they use the term "transference," and he regards
this as a serious handicap. A brief recapitulation of some of the
various views, however, follows.

TRANSFERENCE MODELS

Sandler (1983) remarks that the terms transference and transference resistance, among others, have undergone profound
changes in meaning as new discoveries and new trends have
assumed ascendancy. While Sandler accepts that there are
dimensions of meaning apart from the official definitions, it is
questionable whether there really ever have been such official
definitions of the terms (Cooper 1987). Freud (1905) observed the development of transference in his famous case of
Dora, where the young woman developed positive feelings
toward him in her unconscious. These same feelings were also
reactivated by a family friend, K., and his apparent sexual
approaches to her. Freud believed that it was Dora's difficulties with her unconscious phantasies about him (Freud) that
led her to break off treatment. He originally spoke of the
development of a transference neurosis "when . . . the treatment has obtained mastery over the patient . . . the whole of
his illness' new production is concentrated upon a single
point—his relation to the doctor . . . all the patient's symptoms have abandoned their original meaning and taken on a
new sense which lies in relation to the transference; or only
such symptoms have persisted as are capable of undergoing
such a transformation" (Freud 1917b, p. 444). This picture
has been remarkably transformed by clinical observation.

Freud himself abandoned the term "transference neurosis" later (after 1922), possibly because of the "disparity between the ideal construct and the complex nature of transference-neurotic phenomena and continuation of extra transference manifestations of unconscious intrapsychic conflict" (Blum 1983, p. 589). In *An Outline of Psycho-Analysis* (published posthumously, 1940), where he last comments on the analytic situation, Freud writes:

> The most remarkable thing is this. The patient is not satisfied regarding his analyst in the light of reality as a helper and adviser who, moreover, is remunerated for the trouble he takes and who would himself be content with such a role as that of a guide on a difficult mountain climb. On the contrary, the patient sees in him the return, the reincarnation, of some important figures out of his childhood past and consequently transfers onto him feelings and reactions which undoubtedly apply to this prototype. The fact of transference soon becomes a factor of undreamt-of importance, on the one hand an instrument of irreplaceable value, and on the other a source of serious dangers . . . The analyst may shame-facedly admit to himself that he set out on a difficult undertaking without any suspicion of the extraordinary powers that would be at his command . . .
> . . . Another advantage of transference, too, is that in it the patient produces for us with plastic clarity an important part of his life-story, of which he would probably have given us only an insufficient account. He acts it before us, as it were, instead of reporting it to us. [pp. 174–176]

Freud saw the transference interpretation as a method of strengthening the ego against past unconscious wishes and conflicts.

Gitelson (1952) points out that if the transference is to be a truly irrational recapitulation of childhood relationships, subject to psychoanalytic interpretation, then nothing in the current reality must intervene to give it concurrent validity. This exclusion of everything in the current reality takes no account of unavoidable changes in time, external surroundings, or technique. The implication is that this is not possible.

Broader definitions of the transference are developed by Melanie Klein and her followers (see Segal 1973, who demonstrates the Kleinian view clearly and extensively). In her treatment of children, Klein used toys to reveal the experiences that the child could not express in words to give her a picture of the unconscious objects in the child's inner world. From the Kleinian model and its usage there comes the idea that there is constant projecting by the patient into the analyst, and it is this projecting that is the essence of analysis (Pick 1985). This has serious implications for any therapist treating the depressive symptomatologies: not only can depressed patients put the affects of their depression into their therapists but they *do so continually.* Further, these depressive affects are accompanied by fantasies and phantasies (Kleinians differentiate by the spelling used between the former, which are judged to be conscious, and the latter, which are unconscious, in the internal world).

Meltzer (1981) comments that Freud was bound to view transference as a repetition of the past, and therefore bound to think of neurotics as people "suffering from reminiscences." Freud cannot think of them as people *living* in the past because such a concept could not find any representation in his model (Meltzer 1981). Melanie Klein, Meltzer points out, discovered that we do not live in one world but in two; that we live in an internal world, which is as real a place to live in as is the outside world. This gives a new significance to the concept of phantasy—namely that unconscious phantasies are transactions actually taking place in the internal world. It also leads to a radically altered view of the concept of transference. Instead of transference phenomena being seen as relics of the past, they can now be seen as externalizations of the immediate present, of the internal situation, to be studied as psychic reality. Patients are seen not as suffering from reminiscences but as, in a sense, living in the past, because the past is represented in the immediate present of the internal world at the child or infantile level of mental life. In the Kleinian model, all of these experiences, objects, or part objects can at times be projected into the analyst or therapist.

Meltzer goes on to point out that ego functions can be projected as well, an elaboration of the ideas of Wilfred Bion. Projection, in contrast to projective identification, is putting affects or thoughts into another person, to whom they are then seen as belonging.

Projective identification, first described by Melanie Klein (1952), is somewhat different. An internal object or part of the self, or even the whole self, is projected into an object. The aim may be one of several. It may be primarily to get rid of unwanted parts (as in projection); it may be to possess or control the receiving object, or to attack it, or to avoid separation from it, or any combination of these aims. The result is that the object becomes identified, or partly identified, with the projected part of the self. Projective identification gives rise to misperception of objects. It can give rise to a variety of anxieties, about part of the self being trapped and imprisoned by the object, for example, or depletion of the self through loss of the projected part, or retaliation of the projected object on the self (persecutory delusion and blocking of introjection, which is felt as "projective identification in reverse"). This is regarded as an ongoing process (Segal 1977).

AGE DIFFERENCES

The nature and significance of the transference may to some extent be affected by the age of the patient. Blos (1980), in speaking of adolescents, points out that transferences can be viewed in developmental perspectives relative to first, "the process of adolescent psychic restructuring" and second, "the development tasks inherent in the adolescent process." Blos summarizes "adolescent-specific developmental characteristics" as (1) the second individuation process of adolescence, postulating a normal regression in the service of development (i.e., nondefensive); (2) a biphasic resolution of the Oedipus complex, postulating that the resolution of the Oedipus complex, or the reversed or negative Oedipus complex, is a task of adolescence, thus bringing childhood to a close. He views transference in adolescence as unique and related to the following issues: (1) nondefensive regression, (2) organization of ego continuity (encompassing the personal history), (3) coming to terms with "residual trauma" through character stabilization, and (4) sexual identity formation.

King (1980), on the other hand, describes the transference in middle-aged and elderly patients. Here the transference may take various forms including eroticized or psychotic affects, which may have superimposed on the transference as the result of the impact of unconscious phantasies. These affects, however, are often intense and may arouse in the analyst unacceptable feelings held toward his or her own aging parents.

King remarks on the time limitations set in treatment, both by aging and by financial considerations concomitant with retirement. She cites examples in the transference of patients' denying their actual position in the life cycle and acting-out behavior more reminiscent of adolescence than of middle age. She remarks how difficult it is to terminate the analysis of these patients since they have the fantasy that by avoiding change or therapeutic improvement they will be out of time, and thereby avoid aging and death. These patients may unconsciously link mental health with being alive and have the impression that analysis is keeping them alive.

The above references are taken from psychoanalytic literature, but all of these remarks may be applied directly to patients in psychotherapy in its various forms.

Charles, for example, an elderly man whose case is described more fully in a later chapter, had powerful affects develop in the transference. These were often quite negative because his underlying phantasy, which was brought to the surface of his consciousness to become a conscious fantasy, was that his therapist was the only important external object in his world and served the function of keeping him alive. He also expected the therapist to make arrangements for the care of his two daughters, both adult, as if the therapist were to replace the wife who had died.

NEUTRALITY AND IMPACT

Many of the debates about the nature and use of the transference inevitably call into question the stance of the therapist. Poland (1984) views a therapist's neutrality as a position and one, therefore, to be distinguished from the technical principal of abstinence. Both are active processes. Neutrality means that the analyst (and the therapist) has an openness to all experiences and processes in the patient. Abstinence implies a more narrow limitation of transference gratification in order to promote further psychological work, not giving on the one level in order to facilitate regression to a deeper level of hidden meanings. Poland goes on to suggest that neutrality also implies the therapist's avoidance of imposing his or her self or values on the patient. This includes inhibiting the urge to dominate or have power over the patient. On the contrary, he points out that "it is of primary importance for the analyst to conduct himself so that the analytic process proceeds on the basis of what the patient brings to it. Modesty is thus an essential contribution to recognition that absolute neutral objectivity cannot be fully achieved" (quoting Gitelson 1952, p. 296).

Pick (1985), following the views of Segal (1973), stresses that we are not neutral in the sense of having no reaction, and she goes on to point out that "patients are quite skilled in projecting into particular aspects of the analyst . . . into an analyst's wish to be a mother, the wish to be all-knowing or to deny unpleasant knowledge, into the analyst's instinctual sadism, or into his defences against it. And above all, he projects into the analyst's guilt, or into the analyst's internal objects" (p. 161). This position requires an extended view of the ego, the self, and the unconscious and conscious systems, which needs to be worked out further by Kleinian theorists. All agree, however, that powerful forces are unleashed in the transference in analysis and psychotherapy.

More and more we are beginning to see that many of these powerful forces are in the nonverbal or silent area of the transactions between the patient and the analyst or therapist. McLaughlin (1987) uses "subtle nonverbal cues and accompaniment," which he regards as being rich in allusions to meaning, motivation, and history in the patient. Here we begin to see a broadening of the transference definition to include nonverbal elements, which has important implications. It means that depressive patients (seen in whatever model, classical or contemporary, Freudian, Kleinian, object relations theories, and so on) put important nonverbal messages into their therapists.

Cooper (1987) expresses his concern about therapists' engaging in activities that are excessively self-revelatory or that force the patient into a social relationship. Cooper feels that these forces are much broader than we thought a few years ago. He admits, though, that almost any behavior, including restraint or silence, influences the patient's response, raising the question that it is not easy to know what in the transference are iatrogenic consequences of therapist behavior rather than intrapsychically derived patient behaviors.

WHOSE PROBLEM?

Many therapists have some facility in dealing with the depressed patient, particularly the patient who displays what used to be termed the *reactive depression,* presumably to the loss, real or imagined, of a love object, and reacts aggressively to the internal, introjected, ambivalently loved object, which has been lost and introjected in phantasy. Simple exercises in trying to get the patient to externalize the anger are easy but insufficient.

Richard, a second-year psychiatric resident, had transferred to a psychoanalytically oriented unit, but his previous experience had been using such simple models. He focused his therapy work upon a depressed patient, trying to get the man to verbalize in a forceful manner his reaction to the loss of a girlfriend who had rejected him. Richard did not see the patient's ambivalence, which included love as well as hate, and that within the reactive depression there was always an expression of hope that the object might be retained, returned, or repaired. Richard attempted to get his patient to develop an artificial transference neurosis. His aim was to extend the transference so that the patient would take out his repressed rage upon Richard himself, the therapist. To this end he had the patient performing unpleasant tasks, such as scrubbing the floors of the ward. Richard's supervisor pointed out the element of sadism in his treatment of the patient. He suggested to Richard that this was probably an extension of his feelings about himself and a reaction to previous rejections in his own life—Richard, in fact, had had several mildly verbally sado-masochistic relationships with women—and that the patient had unconsciously maneuvered him into playing a sadistic role. Richard had responded forcibly to depression aroused in him by the patient. This supervisory work seemed to induce guilt in Richard and led to a slightly masochistic deference on his part toward the supervisor. This reaction, in turn, had to be taken up. Further work made Richard realize that the patient's depression was the patient's responsibility, not his. He saw the necessity of the therapists' maintaining a psychological boundary and distance between themselves and their patients. His own overidentification with his patient had led to a stirring up of reminiscences within himself that was untoward.

EMPATHY

Empathy is now a very popular subject, as is "empathic identification" with the patient. The following points, necessary to make here, are in no way an attempt to summarize the vast literature that has been written about these concepts.

Poland (1984) notes the shift in the use of the word empathy from a form of perception to a "global constellation blending perception and response." This shift, he goes on to say, has not been universally accepted and has caused some misunderstandings. He feels that "empathic response" is often used to imply a too readily positive reaction that can interfere with full understanding. He also feels that "rather than exploring the unfolding transference hate, the analyst hurries to repair the presumed basic rent, acting as if he appreciates the underlying hurt that must, he thinks, explain the rage. This assumes that a negative current in the transference neurosis is a defect in the primary transference. Too often the supposedly humane response is a failure of empathic perceptive accuracy" (p. 290). This is likewise true of the depressed patient and of his or her impact upon the therapist.

It is important to understand all the dimensions of the patient's depression rather than to prematurely leap to provide a prescription, be it in the form of reassurance, of a good replacement object, or of drugs.

Jaffe (1986), reviewing the literature on empathy, thinks that there are six general headings that encompass the topic. These are, to summarize: (1) cognitive and affective processes and the role of regression; (2) mother–child origins of empathy; (3) introspection, vicarious introspection, and the knowledgeability of reality; (4) similarities in the subject–object experience; (5) modes of sensorimotor participation; and (6) merging, overidentification, and other problems.

A slightly different view (Chediak 1979) regards empathic identification with the patient as being subsumed under the term counterreaction. He regards the analyst's or therapist's transference to the patient (which is a reliving of early part object relations as elicited by certain features in the patient) and the analyst's or therapist's countertransference (the reaction of the analyst to the role he is assigned by the patient's transference) also as part of the therapist's or analyst's counterreaction.

Arlow (1985) distinguishes between empathy and countertransference. In both there is an identification effected with the patient. In empathy the identification is transient, a temporary sharing of derivative expressions of the patient's unconscious fantasies and wishes. In the case of countertransference, (the therapist) ". . . remains fixed at the point of identification with the patient . . . caught up with the conflicts identical to those of the patient" (p. 166). Arlow feels that many fail to make an adequate distinction between the transient identification that is characteristic of empathy and the persistent identification that leads to countertransference.

Abend (1989) remarks that "empathic listening" has evolved into yet another of those conceptual thickets within which fierce doctrinal battles are being fought (p. 389).

EXPLAINING EMPATHY

Here we see, in my view, some merging of different conceptual systems. How can empathy occur except by projective identification, by, that is to say, part of the therapist's psyche being put temporarily into the patient? That part of the therapist's psyche then looks internally at the patient's internal world and externally toward the patient's external objects. The therapist's parts are then taken back into him- or herself, thereby bringing understanding of what the patient is experiencing.

Turquet (1975) shows how extensively everyone uses projective identification and, its counterpart, introjection (the internalization of projected bits of the psyches of others). This is a continuous process. We "feel other people out" unconsciously, unintentionally, rapidly, when we first meet them and this "feeling out" is part of our ongoing relationship. "Empathic identification," therefore, is a constant process rather than a simply therapeutic one, which develops in therapy and which fluctuates. The usual empathy of everyday life also fluctuates: we distance ourselves or close ourselves to certain people; others are brought closer. Relationships occur. We like some and dislike others. Sometimes what we see in them is the introjection of our own projective identification evaluatory bits back into ourselves.

Self psychologists (Bacal and Newman 1990) suggest that empathy is tuning in to the emotional state of the other and distinguishing or deconfusing the two, while projective identification involves whole or part identification with the other. It could be argued equally that such tuning in involves putting oneself temporally into the other to see what he or she feels like—which is projective identification and then re-introjection. Their term "deconfusing" implies a conscious process. Projective identification, back and forth between patient and therapist, explains the intersubjective field concept of self psychology.

VIEWS ON COUNTERTRANSFERENCE

Freud (1910) comments on "the countertransference which arises in the physician as a result of the patient's influence on his unconscious feelings" (p. 144) and counsels the analyst to begin his activity with self-analysis. Later (1915) he refers specifically to transference love. He remarks that some therapists may wish to try to get the patient to suppress, renounce, or sublimate some instincts. This, he asserts, would be an unanalytic way of dealing with them and a senseless one. To do anything other than analyze would be not only technically wrong but foolish. He uses, as Chediak (1979) reminds us, the analogies of the mirror and the surgeon: the mirror reflects to the patient what he is doing and saying, the surgeon uses his scalpel to cut through to the unconscious. Freud tries to convey the need to keep the analyst's private life, feelings, and thoughts from affecting the dyad, to influence it as little as possible. This is the classic view.

Chediak, commenting that we are unable to agree what countertransference is, discusses whether it should be viewed as a noxious development or a valuable tool of treatment. He talks of dividing the global counterreaction into cognitive–affective counterreactions having two possible origins, namely (a) knowledge of the patient based on an understanding of the patient's verbal descriptions and nonverbal communications, put together with the help of theory as a temporary hypothesis and (b) the counterreaction, which is directly related to the dyadic analyst–analysand relations. Chediak feels that within this division are four components that overlap and are not easily identified: (1) the analyst's reaction to the patient as a person, to his character structure, conflicts, assets and liabilities, his social, cultural, religious, and financial qualities; (2) the analyst's empathic identification; (3) countertransference: the analyst's reaction to the role he is assigned by the patient's transference; and (4) the analyst's transference to the patient. In this the patient's psychopathology has been relegated to a secondary place by his having revived, by certain of his features, the analyst's transference potential, derived from the analyst's own early part object relationships.

Arlow (1985) discusses persistent countertransference identifications. He feels that the classic blind spot, the "refusal" or inability to "see" what the material is about, is one form of response—and this is, in his view, the most frequent factor in such blind spots. What is happening is that the analyst does not want the patient's material to remind him or her of his or her own unconscious conflicts. Analysts miss the interpretation, therefore, or fail to give it, and justify their reluctance by various rationalizations. They may even attempt to divert the patient.

A second form of response arises from the nature of the material. It may evoke fantasy wishes not necessarily identified with the unconscious wishes of the patient. These may be complimentary—as in the case of the patient's wish to be rescued and the wish of the analyst to rescue. Material quite peripheral to the patient's central conflicts may have an evocative effect upon the analyst's potential for countertransference.

A third is when there is something in the situation that is evocation of the analyst's conflicts. The analyst may play out some unconscious role of being the central performer. He may, for example, display his cleverness by using the situation as a testing ground for his capabilities, or he may assume the role of an admiring auditor, unconsciously identifying with the patient. The physical situation may stimulate unconscious wishes connected with passivity, masochism, and so forth.

At this point it might be useful to turn to the contributions of Heimann (1959). Heimann points out that the term now includes what is perceived and self-analyzed, not in order to overcome the countertransference but to put it in the service of the analyst's understanding, to use it to comprehend what is happening between the two persons present in the session. What seems to be now taken as a given was at the time a considerably controversial point.

Kernberg (1965) discusses the two contrasting approaches to the concept of countertransference. The first, called the "classical" one, stays close to the use proposed by Freud. The second approach is termed a "totalistic" one, and is one in which the countertransference is viewed as a total emotional reaction to the patient.

Racker (1948) asserts that the whole of the patient's personality, the healthy part, the neurotic part, his past and present, reality and phantasy, are brought into play in his relationship with the analyst: so it is with the analyst, though with qualitive and quantitive differences, in his relation with the patient. Neither is free of neurosis. Psychic conflicts remain unresolved and strive for a solution. Professional, social, and financial situations are also subject to the transference. Finally, the direct relation with the patient itself leads to a transference, because the analyst's choice of a profession, like all choices, is based upon the object relations of infancy. Racker calls the whole of the analyst's images, feelings and impulses toward the patient, insofar as they are determined by the past, countertransference, and the pathological expression of this may be denominated "countertransference neurosis."

Waksman (1986), commenting upon the differences in reaction to the use of countertransference between the classicists and the totalists, feels that the former group regard countertransference as if it were a sin and the latter may use the term as counteridentification. Racker, Waksman says, would regard it as projective counteridentification, and that, in his view, would be Grinsberg's response.

Silverman (1985) suggests that one dimension of the subject that has received insufficient attention is that the analysand, in turn, uses his or her intuitive and empathic abilities to detect evidence of emotional conflicts in the analyst. Silverman talks about the impressive ability of certain patients to subtly and skillfully produce desired feelings in reactive responses by their analysts.

This raises serious questions, but ones that can again be explained in terms of an extended model of the transference-
-countertransference situation. Patients, by empathic identification, also put psychic parts of themselves into their therapists, and take these back as a way of sounding out what is going on. By doing this they can get a "picture" of what is going on within the conscious and unconscious of their therapist. Most do this intuitively and spontaneously. We also see situations in which the supervisee repeats with his or her supervisor some of the defenses that the patient exhibits. This is an excellent example of projective identification, of what the patient has created in his or her therapist that is re-created in the supervision.

Balint, in his work with general practitioners in London, England, observed that the group of physicians would replicate in the case discussions some of the hidden object relations of the patient being discussed, as reported by the general practitioner to his group of peers. Thus an extended view of the countertransference allows the use of counterreactions to the patient to be an excellent diagnostic tool.

ADDING DIMENSIONS

What is left out in these discussions is that many of these transference factors are unconsciously perceived by the analyst or therapist, and it is only by evaluating his or her own feelings about the patient that they can be discerned. From this it follows that it is crucially important that the therapist or analyst constantly monitor his or her feelings and fantasies as an ongoing process in every therapy. How many or how much of them are his or her own or, *equally important* but minimized by some of the literature, to what extent are they introjections of the patient's projective identifications? That is to say, the feelings within the analyst may, in fact, have been put into him by the patient in a projective identificatory way. In the same way, the fantasies within him or her may not be the therapist's own, but may be the result of unconscious phantasies projected into him or her, which have then aroused fantasies in the therapist's conscious or preconscious.

One can differentiate the various components of the analyst's or therapist's experience. Doing so allows for clarity of communication. It clarifies the role, and the concept of neutrality that should be aimed at, and it helps delineate objectively between the patient psychopathology and the analyzing function, and potential for reactivation, of the therapist's or analyst's psychopathology. It also refutes the misleading assumption that all the problems re-created in the analytic process belong at all times to the patient. My concern about the latter point is that it is *too easy to overlook the continuing, ongoing, projective identifications into the therapist or analyst.*

Chediak (1979) has some valuable points. He gives warning, for example, of the situation where conflicts interfere with the ability to treat the patient. He advises establishing a rationale for limiting self-disclosures to the patient. He warns against the dangers of overreaction to the patient. But unless one takes an extended model of countertransference, then, in my view, valuable information about the ongoing therapy is missed. Chediak emphasizes that while he has been referring mainly to the psychoanalytic dyad, the same concepts regarding counterreaction apply to psychoanalytically oriented psychotherapy, group psychotherapy, hospital psychiatry, the treatment of borderline and schizophrenic patients, and family therapy. I would concur with this, but would also add that projective identification occurs continually and should be noted in all these circumstances too, including case discussions of hospitalized patients, and the relation of them and the nursing team (who constitute a psychological group). Patients project parts of their psyche into various members of the care-giving team, into occupational and rehabilitational therapists, social workers, and so on. These parts are introjected in differing ways by members of such teams. They may be reacted to. Furthermore, they may be reacted to as if they are spontaneous responses by, say, the nurse, rather than projective identificatory parts of the patient; parts that might give signals about the patient's feelings, fantasies, or phantasies (the former being conscious, the latter unconscious, both of which can still be projected).

WOUNDED HEALERS

Nothing in what I wish to say should take away from my view that severely disturbed or psychotic people should not enter into any procedure to become psychotherapists or psychoanalysts. Such persons may be attracted by the mental health professions since they often search for internal healing and self-understanding, often in a magical way. Moreover, nothing I say about how therapists are made "wounded" by patients takes away from the need that a screening process be part of the selection of candidates for the various psychotherapy training programs. I would hold that this is necessary for all kinds of therapist, and ideally for all who would enter any of the mental health professions, for psychiatric nurses, psychiatric occupational therapists, psychiatric social workers, and the like. Personal psychotherapy or psychoanalysis is recommended in order that one may see how one responds to patients and how one's own personality reacts and interacts. Nevertheless, a therapist's very problems may make for an empathic identification with patients or clients, and for an understanding that makes the therapist a better one.

Waksman (1986) quotes the views of Wender about the choice of vocation: "It is the perception of the call or demand of the internalized object which may ask for, demand, claim, beg for attention, care, reconstruction, reparation . . . for the damage, thoughtless or (by) manipulations to which it has been subject" (p. 409). Wender goes on: "Vocation may be understood as the impulse to give coherent and appropriate expression to the reparatory requirements which have arisen in response to the unconscious perception of the damaged internal object. This is involved in the . . . working through of the anxieties corresponding to the depressive position." Waksman raises the interesting question: does countertransference arise from the unconscious conflicts of the analyst or from his nonconflictual unconscious wishes? Or does it arise out of his reality needs, as Kernberg asserts? Waksman feels it is unnecessary to make this distinction because the boundaries are so tenuous. In any case we see somewhat wounded healers attempting to deal with much more severely wounded patients or clients.

Waksman discusses the problems arising from the identification by the therapist with the child or the parent or the reality needs in a particular case. My own view would be slightly different in that, if such an identification occurs, is it aroused by the projective identicatory parts of the patient of child or parent, or the reality needs that are then projected into the therapist or analyst by the patient or client, an important distinction.

Racker (1948) was one of the early analysts who pointed out the massive effects that the even "ordinary" patient can have upon the "ordinary" analyst. This also applies to therapists of all persuasions. Intense feelings are aroused in psychotherapy, particularly in that of an intensive or in-depth nature.

Ferenczi (1919) emphasizes the difficulty of dealing si-

multaneously with the interpretation of the transference and
of the analyst's countertransference. Again, considering the
neutrality of the analyst, he remarks that an excessive reti-
cence on the part of the analyst may give rise to a coldness,
which increases resistance in the patient and may cause him or
her to break off treatment. Ferenczi talks about the difficulty
of striking a proper balance between what the analyst should
show the patient and what he or she should keep to himself.
He does, however, recommend that the psychoanalyst express him- or herself openly on occasion. This was and is still
yet another controversial question. Often a therapist may
make an inappropriate remark, an expression of a personal
view, say, to a patient and may later regret it. Withdrawal into
guilt by the therapist or self-moralizing, however, may cause
an even greater disruption of the therapeutic process. In any
event, intense feelings are aroused in therapists and may affect
them directly. Margaret Little (1951) points out that acting
out the countertransference is unnecessary or ill-timed.

Blum (1983) draws attention to the analyst's irrational
reactions to the work of analysis itself as well as to all aspects
of the patient, and to the impact that events in the analyst's life
may have upon countertransference potentials. In most case
discussions these background effects are rarely admitted, except in a most general way. They are often embarrassing
things to discuss, and therefore a discussant usually finds a
modification of them for public presentation.

UNDERSTAND REACTIONS

Whereas countertransference, including one's counterreactions to the patient and one's recognition of the projections put
into one by the patient, is valuable in treatment, I am opposed to the disclosure of "countertransference" to the patient
except on the rare occasions when such disclosure might

further treatment. However, spontaneous disclosures are often made. A subsequent look at the transactions between therapist and patient, which may be extremely valuable, may then ensue. Self-analysis or self-inspection may reveal that the disclosure was a response to the unconscious projected bits that were put into the therapist by the patient, or, conversely, to the patient by the therapist, experiencing a small and short-term internal psychological disruption. The disclosure, an apparent "accident," therefore, may be very valuable to both parties in terms of the analysis of what happened thereafter.

Almost at the end of a session, I once found myself rummaging around my desk for a catalogue of psychiatric books and I had the fantasy that I was behaving like a picker of garbage bins. Quite unintentionally, I remarked to the patient that I was behaving like a picker of garbage, rummaging around. I watched a severely deprived patient burst into sobbing. At the next session, when he tried to avoid dealing with this, I reminded him of the end of the previous session, and we discussed the intensity of the transference to me, which he had been trying to conceal. My inadvertent apparent "mistake" was due to the nature of the transference, and the patient projecting into me that which he felt about his father. Most of the gifts the father had given him were those the father had got from picking up the leftovers of other people. As a child, the patient could not equate this with the family's straitened circumstances but could only see the things as other people's rejects. Late in his analysis he came to see them, instead, as emotionally valuable gifts from his father to him, which had helped him through some of the deprived phases of his childhood. My remark about my activity of "rummaging," therefore, was a response to how he had projected into me, by projective identification an image of his father. Fortunately I recognized this. I appeared to have been turned almost completely, psychologically, into his father. But it was a loving act to do this. The patient was afraid internal feelings of love would be destroyed by internal ones of hate, so that he tended to project his love into others for safekeeping, including into me in the analysis. My remarks were, in fact, a reminder of interest in him, and of the loving his father had given him. What was at first glance a mistake, and could have been taken to indicate that he thought our work was garbage, was interpreted a different way: he needed to relive through me the experience of his father's care and gifts when his mother had been away.

My concern is that some of the moralistic aspects of our culture and, indeed, of our upbringing has come, inadvertently, into much of our training and clinical work. Reading the reports of supervision or listening to trainees agonize over their cases suggests that we have in no way ameliorated the harshness of the superegos in so many of us. Rather than focusing only upon limits, in whatever form of therapy training, it might be equally useful to show trainees the meaning of their mistakes and to help them to look themselves at the meaning of such mistakes, past, present, and future, and their effects upon the patient or client. They might be encouraged to consider the effects of the unconscious of all the parties, including the supervisor, in the relationships. It should again be emphasized that the supervisor is not free of the projections of the patient, which are put into his therapist, who in turn reprojects them into the supervisor. The supervisor, by his scrutiny of the effects of the patient upon himself, can play a valuable role.

Carolyn, a therapist who was also in a personal analysis, became overwhelmed by the difficulties of treating 8-year-old Tommy, largely, she said, because she could not handle the pleading, depressive behavior of Tommy's mother, with whom she had sessions once a week. Carolyn became quite depressed. For a few sessions she, in turn, depressed *her* analyst, whose initial reaction was to offer to supervise her on her case. Fortunately, after a while, he recognized what was happening in the analytic relationship. He made interpretations about the multiple projections into Carolyn and into himself from Carolyn as a result of her overload. These insights helped her see that not only was Tommy depressed by some things that were going on in his family, which warranted further exploration, but he was also further depressed by his mother's reactive depression to his psychological disturbances. Carolyn's therapeutic investigation revealed that the primary casualty in the family she was treating was Tommy's father, who had hardly been mentioned hitherto, who was protected by the mother and the child. The father had severe mental problems and was, in turn, thought to be severely depressed.

It would have been easy for the analyst to feel guilty for having been depressed by Carolyn. Carolyn, in turn, felt guilty about apparently having succumbed to her patient's depressive effect upon her. She ruminated about her capacity to do therapeutic work. She recalled early childhood conflicts, anxieties about ability and schoolwork. She reexperienced childhood depressions. The analyst was reminded of his own childhood, and of his own early days as a psychotherapist, concerned about every mistake. From the perspective of an extended view of the transference–countertransference we can see the enlightenment that could be gained by considering the hidden, but massive and multiple, projective identifications that were going on. Tommy was the designated "casualty" in the malfunctioning family. The depressed father put his depression into his son. His wife, Tommy's mother, depressed about her depressed husband, did the same. The depressed boy was brought to therapy.

In therapy Tommy's guilt about his phantasies about damaging his father and his depression about this were brought to the surface. Carolyn recognized the family's modes of projective identification and guilt. She had been made to feel depressed and guilty, just as Tommy was. In turn she had, temporarily, made her analyst feel depressed and guilty and, to cope with this, he had supervised her case—until he realized that his action was a reaction to what had been done to him. His insight led him to make interpretations to Carolyn, who was then able to see, and to make Tommy understand, that he was the carrier of his father's and his mother's problems for which, despite his magical phantasies that he had contributed to them, he was not responsible.

NEUTRALITY PROBLEMS

Poland (1984) discusses the untoward effect of excessive neutrality. He tells of a young analyst presenting a case fragment about a troubled young woman who could not afford a babysitter, but daily locked her 5-year-old son in a small room, unattended, so that she could go to her sessions. The colleagues in the case discussion, alert to the statements about the child's increasing problems, responded with horror, and the young analyst explained that he felt his task was not to feel guilty but to analyze. In fact, he never had questioned or commented to the patient about the peculiar arrangements. Poland feels that in the guise of neutrality, the young analyst had become a silent partner.

From the traditional view of countertransference, this is an excellent point. From the perspective of the extended view of countertransference that I am proposing, it might well be that the patient was projecting in a nonverbal way her needs for internal controlling mechanisms, certain ego functions about reality, and conflict over these, into the young analyst. He, in turn, projected these into his colleagues and supervisor in the case conference, who experienced intense horror and urges to intervene, which were part of the patient's hidden unconscious as well. The young mother had put them into her analyst, who reprojected them into the case conference, where the conflict was reenacted. It would be appropriate for the young analyst to take up the so-called reality as part of the patient's hidden conflict behind her "locking up" behavior. The patient's projective identifications were carried and re-projected by the presenter into the group members of the case discussion. Horror, guilt, and the need for ego functions and ego assessment of reality may have been in the *unconscious* of the patient and could not be dealt with, but her anxiety over her internal conflicts were unconsciously projected into the young analyst. He reprojected these because he could not, like her, deal with her guilt and horror, or her guilt and horror within him, which he put into his colleagues. These might very well be the patient's unconscious guilt and horror as well as the ego functions of what exactly was called for, for the care of her child. An explanation of these various projections might lead to a reinterpretation by the young analyst of how the patient was using him to "carry" some of the feelings about her child she could not get in touch with, and what to do.

This is a different way of handling this case. Such a different approach to supervision might broaden the young analyst's capacity to use himself as a register and measurer of the rapid to and fro of an analytic or therapeutic situation. It would be interesting to see how object relations in a patient might be re-created in a group discussing the case with this different approach.

FURTHER EXTENSIONS

Silverman (1985) feels that the appearance in the therapist of boredom, sleepiness, vague malaise, irritability, excessive positive or negative feelings toward the patient or about the patient's past and present objects, difficulties in grasping the meaning of communications, dreams about, parapraxes, and various forms of acting out of neurotic inclinations are all signs that something is awry. He adds that a less obvious sign can be the failure of the analysis to progress satisfactorily despite seemingly proper technique and seemingly accurate understanding.

Abend (1989) raises interesting questions as to why the concept of countertransference has been enlarged. He believes that one factor is the introduction of structural theory. Theories about the complexities of unconscious mental functioning include what is really meant by neutrality, and how unconscious elements of defense and superego contribute to intrapsychic conflicts.

A second factor, Abend feels, is the controversies that have arisen over technical principles, including Ferenczi's advocacy of an active technique, which were challenges to Freud's opinions about not influencing the patient's neurosis except through interpretation. Abend cites these changes in Europe and South America by the followers of Klein and the British Middle or Independent Group, as it is now called, who were stimulated by her work, and in the United States by the work of Harry Stack Sullivan and his adherents.

A third factor, Abend suggests, is the application of psychoanalytic technique to the treatment of borderline, severely narcissistic, and psychotic individuals. In treating these patients, Abend contends, it is of prime importance that the analyst or therapist attend to his or her reactions to the patient. Abend also feels that the disillusionment and de-idealization of traditional authority that have characterized our social and intellectual climate since World War II have modified views of the countertransference so that they are less elitist and rigidly authoritarian in spirit than was the classical interpretation.

Jacobs (1973) talks of the idiosyncracies, both in style and in sources, from which the analyst can proceed to analyze him- or herself and thus how each analyst, like each patient, is different from another.

Chediak (1979) points out that empathic identification means identifying with the patient relived in the patient's transference. This identification is of short duration and necessitates an objective evaluation of one's own reaction as part of the therapeutic relationship. With countertransference, on the other hand, the therapist identifies with an object in the patient's past, which was an object relation to the patient and is being reexperienced in the here and now. Thus the analyst's similar experiences are to react to fulfil the patient's needs of that object relationship. This identification can be temporary, alternate or coincide with an objective evaluation, but can also be of long duration. Alternatively, the patient can reactivate conflict in the analyst, which is transference to the patient, and in so doing, obliterate the analyst's analyzing capabilities. When this happens something has gone wrong, and self-analysis, more analysis or therapy, and introspection on the part of patient and therapist are crucial. Unfortunately, sometimes therapy comes to an abrupt stop at this point. This does not mean, necessarily, that the patient will leave but rather that the patient and therapist will continue in a mutually collusive but nonfunctioning situation (Chediak 1979).

PSYCHOLOGICAL "FIT"

The social changes through which we are living have sensitized us to the need to take into account the gender of the therapist or analyst. Rathling and Chused (1988) have discussed cross-gender transferences in four analyst–patient dyads. They find that the gender of the analyst contributes greatly to the transference experience. This does not mean that cross-gender therapy should not be carried out, but rather that the differences should be considered and worked with. The literature in this area is becoming extensive. In some cases, some of the traditional complexes, such as that of a male developing active phallic impulses toward a woman in a position of authority such as that of a female therapist, may be worked out upon another external female person, representing an internal object. All this can be brought into the therapy.

It does, however, follow that some therapists, because of their own internal objects and external object world, cannot treat some people. It is possible, for example, that some male therapists with traditional views of female roles might find it difficult to deal with women who are struggling to break through the traditional constraints upon them. Conversely, it is easy to mistake what might be new "normal" female behavior as a woman's ordinary struggle for her personal right to individuality and not look at the hidden meanings that might be behind this.

THE WORK OF BION

One of the most attractive concepts of early infancy and its development is that of Bion, who draws attention to the importance of projective identification in infancy. He believes that the infant can project into his mother his or her anxiety or aggression, and evoke from her an appropriate response. Bion develops the concept that the infant projects into the breast as a container. The mother's unconscious evaluation of these projections or her reverie, in a nonverbal way, changes meaningless beta-elements into meaningful alpha-elements as an ongoing process. The baby, for example, might project unbearable feelings into the mother, who would make appropriate responses to the baby's behavior. The baby would then introject the breast as a container capable of dealing with such fear and anxiety. The child then has an internal container (equals breast), which becomes the basis of his or her own development of the ability to contain. All of this is subsumed in Bion's concept of the container and the contained (Bion 1962). Bion seems to define alpha-elements as ordinary kinds of objects or emotions, but as Wisdom (1987) indicates, what exactly is an alpha- and a beta-element is not made clear. Supposedly, beta-objects are outside an object, and Bion seems to regard them as sensorydata (sometimes connected with feces). The infant begins life with beta-elements, which constitute its world and have to be translated into alpha-elements. Wisdom complains that Bion does not theorize about how this transition takes place: how an idea is transformed from its state at one time to its state at another, or about "invariance" (with the same basic structure in both cases or phases, that is). Because these elements do not transform into alpha with "invariance," there is a hiatus in the theory. The mother is said to effect this transformation by her reverie (neither the meaning nor the process is clear). Likewise, so do analysts and therapists unconsciously process nonverbal elements from their patients.

Thorner (1981) also talks of the breast as a container of the baby's projections, by which means the indigestible facts or beta-elements become digested and transformed into alpha-elements. Hanna Segal adds that dreams enable beta-elements to become alpha. This assertion also bothers Wisdom (1987).

Whatever shortcomings Wisdom, a philosopher, might find in the theory, which, after all, is an attempt to apprehend a preverbal state, most therapists who learn of it find it a useful one. This makes it warrant further discussion. What is Bion saying exactly? And what are his implications?

USING BION'S VIEWS

Perhaps Bion is talking about what Winnicott called the "holding function" of the mother–baby relationship, which is unconsciously repeated in psychotherapy or psychoanalysis. In psychotherapy or psychoanalysis the patient is given a

psychological structure or "holding and facilitating environment," which will allow him or her to open up in a free
atmosphere and to regress. Many have argued that having a
sympathetic listener is therapeutic in itself. Following from
Bion, it is possible that in some therapies a good "facilitating
environment" is being provided where, on a constant basis,
patients can come and deal in a regressive fashion with their
primitive fantasies, including those that are unconscious. In
the most supportive of therapies, many of these are worked
through and returned to the patient, sometimes in a verbalized
form, sometimes in a nonverbal way. A nonverbal exchange
may have something to do with the therapist's mental processing (including reverie) of unconscious, vague, and complex issues that the patient puts into him or her on a projective
identification basis.

This follows from Bion's concept of the container within
the child, which is one of enormous value. Therapists, likewise, have their own infancy and, therefore, their own container, which is an introject from their own mother–child
relationships.

Where in the internal world of their therapists or analysts
do all the projections and projective identificatory parts of
patients go? Once again the formulations are not clear, but
somewhere within the ego, utilizing both the conscious and
unconscious parts, there is some kind of container or recep-
tacle that allows these projective identificatory parts to be
carried, recognized by another split-off part of the ego or self
for evaluation and response (the synthetic function of the ego
in ego-psychology terms).

Part of the ego has an ego-observing function, which is
fully conscious. Another part is unconscious. This responds to
the unconscious or preconscious parts of the self or ego that
are responding to the patient, and also to the patient's projective identificatory bits into the therapist's ego "container" or
receiver.

As we have said, Melanie Klein has presented a radically different view of the transference. Instead of transference phenomena being seen as relics of the past, she sees them as externalizations of the immediate present of the internal situation, to be studied as psychic reality. "Patients are not seen to be suffering from reminiscences but are, in a sense, to be seen as living in the past, as the past is represented in the immediate present in the internal world at the child or infantile level of mental life" (Meltzer 1981, p. 179).

Bion went on to describe some of the implications of his concept of the container and the contained. The contained might be crushed by the container, the contents might explode the container, but the container and the contained have an adaptive response. We are concerned when the projective identifications of depressive psychic parts overwhelm the container, and cross boundaries into other parts of the ego (into the synthetic parts, say) and even the superego (causing, say, intense internal harsh self-criticism).

To turn momentarily from the effects of depressive fantasies and feelings and their effect upon therapists, let us look at the projective identification of ego functions into therapists.

Cecily was an extraordinarily intelligent and highly educated postgraduate student. She developed an interest in psychoanalytic theory and began to study the biographies of Freud and other major analysts and to relate some of the theory development to the personal biographies of the theorist concerned, with fascinating and impressive results.

As a result of her work, her analyst found that his own cognitive functions were intensified. He experienced a heightened capacity to see similarities and differences he had not seen before, not only in his clinical work but in other parts of his theoretical work, which were totally unrelated to the material the patient was presenting. There may be several explanations for this, but one is that because of a positive transference that caused the patient to pair with him as her long-sought partner, at times she projected into her analyst with great intensity a relatively conflict-free part of her own ego. The analyst went away from the sessions enhanced, carrying with him not only her particular insights but her free approach to many complex theoretical issues.

In the same way, Bion's concept of a container (a conceptualization about what is, presumably, an ego function) has had a liberating effect upon many therapists who use it. Whatever a priori assumptions there are in the concept, it is a useful one. By carrying some of the depression and bizarre fantasies of their patients, therapists may be performing a function akin to that which Bion describes. Similarly, while in dealing with a patient's sense of futility we may stir up our own doubts about the meaning of our existence, the concept allows us to recognize that we are carrying something for the patient. At times we may function as an auxiliary ego.

Countertransference also involves the therapist's putting his or her psychic parts into the patient, or is a reaction to the parts the patient puts into the therapist. The use of projective identification into patients, with the subsequent reintrojection of the patient's parts back, allows many therapists to have a good rapport with patients suffering from all the kinds of depressive symptomatology described in the second chapter of this book, and to treat these patients extremely well. When the therapist becomes identified with the patient, on the other hand, something has gone awry. The therapist may have overempathized with him or her. When the therapist reacts or overreacts to what the patient is doing, there may be *insufficient* empathy, and a conscious or unconscious withholding of projective identification with the patient (and subsequent introjection, taking back, of his or her psychic parts). The therapist may react to the patient's projection of affects, becoming, say, depressed by the patient's projection of depression. This happens when there is a blurring of internal psychological boundaries in the therapist between the cognitive parts of the ego, conscious and unconscious, which are receptive, and the synthetic or thinking part, which deals with what has been received. This breaking of internal boundaries may be a counterreaction to extensive projective identification of, for example, depressive affects and phantasies by the patient into a normally well-functioning therapist.

Many therapists who suffer forms of depressive symptomatology at various times in their lives, however, can have empathic understanding of their patients or clients. This involves the process of putting parts of themself into the patient and seeing the patient's internal world and objects and external world simultaneously, listening to and understanding the patient without losing personal internal or external boundaries. At times in my professional life I have seen colleagues seemingly overwhelmed by various depressive processes as a result of breakups of relationships, personal illness, illness of loved ones, and so on. Some have had recourse to a return to therapy or analysis. In some cases, the depression has enhanced their therapeutic work—and the work itself has bolstered the therapist's sense of self. Involvement with the reality of the patients' needs has prevented further regression in the therapist temporarily traumatized by life events. "Wounded healers" may, in some cases, have a more empathic understanding of their patients or clients and do better work than they might otherwise.

4

Depression Caused by Others: the Patient and the Therapist

Sometimes it is regarded as a therapeutic necessity to be caught in a patient's psychosis or turbulence. Searles (1965), for example, does so in his work in the psychotherapy of schizophrenia. To respond to a patient with a conscious or unconscious counterreaction is part of the ongoing process in such psychotherapy. Thus, the sexual fantasies and fantasies of violence evoked by these patients are understood to be part of the therapist's working life. Presumably these feelings and fantasies are conscious, or are made so by the self-analysis that is a continuing part of our therapeutic work. To respond without action to seductive or provocative behavior by the patient in the therapeutic setting suggests an intuitive and understanding therapist. To be depressed by a patient's depression, however, seems to be a far less desirable response. Yet all of us remark how depressing certain individuals are.

We guard against depressing people by the usual defenses of violence, disavowal, repression, and denial, and by the manic defenses of triumph, control, and contempt (Segal

69

1973). Other avoidance behavior includes reinforcing the depressed person's omnipotent defenses by reassuring him or her that there will be a replacement for the lost loved one, that the person who did the abandoning was not really worth it, and so on. Patients who cannot cope with their depression are sometimes met with contempt, as they are in their everyday lives. Why, then, do therapists not deal with such defensive responses to depression in the consulting room?

PROJECTIVE IDENTIFICATION

The concept of projective identification, as we have said, was developed originally by Klein (see Segal 1973) and is useful in the psychoanalytic understanding both of individual patients and of groups and social systems. Projective identification means that part of the self is put unconsciously into another person, so that there is the feeling of being in the other's psyche in various ways. The mother dressing her daughter for the wedding, for example, puts "parts of herself" into her daughter and thereby enjoys and lives out the role of the bride vicariously through her daughter. The daughter unconsciously introjects, or takes in, part of her mother and allows this to happen. The mother feels, unconsciously, that part of herself is in the bride, providing guidance and control. The daughter, for her part, may very strongly feel her mother in her, and feel directed by her.

Projection, on the other hand, involves externalizing a part of oneself, usually a thought or feeling, putting it into another, then perceiving it coming back at oneself.

Turquet (1975), as we have seen, elaborates on the concept of projective identification, and the corresponding introjection, and moves the concept into the role of reality testing. Turquet suggests that projective identification occurs in almost all situations. When individuals meet they put part of themselves into each other, then take it back to get the feel of what the other person is really about. This is done rapidly, spontaneously, and unconsciously. Similarly, in small groups we instantly put parts of ourselves into the other members and then take these back, so that we get a feel for those we are dealing with in the group. We do this in both clinical and social situations.

Bion (1962) emphasizes that therapists, too, are containers for projective identificatory bits, and that it is important for them to recognize what is being done to them. This is invaluable in the understanding of patients. We must deal with the nonverbal aspects of patients from the moment they come into the consulting room, transmitting in a nonverbal, unconscious way what is going on within themselves. Therapists may consciously formulate interpretations or interventions in response to what the patient says, verbally or nonverbally, but in addition, there are cues that we transmit to the patient as a human response to what the patient is doing to us.

Bion's concept (discussed in the previous chapter) of the mother receiving disorganized bits of the infant's psyche, processing these raw elements, and returning them to the baby in a way that is nonverbal but that "creates" sense in the infant, may suggest an explanation as to why many different sorts of therapies are effective. Many patients report that one of the most important things a therapist has done for them is just "be there." It is possible that this "being there" has involved subtle, nonverbal transmissions between patient and therapist—the mere physical presence of a therapist is insufficient explanation of a therapeutic result—consciously or unconsciously reminiscent of the roles of mother and child.

Another aspect of the concept of the therapist as a container may be developed from Bion's theory of the container and the contained. In the therapy of adults one of the functions of the therapist is to receive the verbal and nonverbal

affective aspects that the patient transmits, hold them, often
for several sessions, and then reflect back to the patient what
has been happening. This conscious reflection also contains a
processing of the content of the patient's account of a particular part of his or her history. In this way the therapist as
container carries, often for a period of time, and processes,
both consciously and unconsciously, the patient's affects, ac-
counts, fantasies (conscious), and phantasies (unconscious).

PROJECTIVE IDENTIFICATION AND MIRRORING

It is possible that the understanding of how we all require
mirroring for our self-maintenance, provided by self-psy-
chology, may also be arrived at by an elaboration of Bion's
concept. It may be that the patient not only requires mirroring
from people or inanimate objects or situations that represent
self-objects, but endows these with unconscious projective
identificatory parts of his or her psyche. These are assumed to
be processed by the other person, and the patient then introjects the reprocessed parts and thereby feels gratification,
harmony, cohesiveness, and so on of the self, a process that is
termed "mirroring." Thus mirroring is done better by a
human being than by inanimate objects or situations. The
function of the other person as a self-object is to consciously
make statements related to the patient or his or her activities,
but unconscious processing of the patient may be involved as
well.

THE "SELECTED" PATIENT

Projective identification explains the phenomenon of scape-
goating seen in families and in groups. A particular individual

in a family is "selected" unconsciously to "carry," for example, the delinquency of all the others, to act out the rebellion, and so on. Sometimes the scapegoat is made into the family failure and, usually at the same time, the family member who is depressed on behalf of the others. In the same way, in groups, particular individuals are selected unconsciously to play particular roles or object relationships. The "failures" in group work or therapy may "carry" the failure and depression not only for themselves but for the other group members as well.

Susan, a 30-year-old woman, was married but unsuccessful in getting pregnant and experienced subsequent depressive crises. She was the older daughter of a prominent family of lawyers who placed much emphasis upon success and themselves had proven competence in their selected fields. Father was reputed to be a brilliant criminal laywer and mother a brilliant corporate one. While high achievers, both were reported at times to be hypochondriacal; mother was reported to be depressed.

Susan seemed to be regarded as a particular failure, as both had wished for a boy. They rejoiced at the birth of their second child, their long-sought son, who was endowed with all the capabilities for a success he subsequently achieved, at least on the surface.

Susan reported that she had been periodically depressed all her life. In adolescence, she handled this by overeating, which only made the family regard her as more of a failure within their social system. In her treatment, of course, it emerged that her overeating was an appeal for love and nurture, accompanied by certain provocative aspects. Nevertheless, she was constantly regarded in a derisory way by both her father and mother. Susan chose to study history. Her intellectual brilliance became apparent and she was supported by her peer group and by her family, since academia was considered an alternative route to the professions.

The brother studied law, successfully, to his parents' joy, though he confessed to his sister that he hated the work. Since he believed these negative feelings were unacceptable, he minimized them when speaking with his parents.

One saw how, within the family, Susan had been brought up to be an unwanted object. Her treatment revealed how she longed for a penis, and was narcissistically vulnerable to attacks upon her body image and her intellectual competence. As a result Susan had come to regard herself as a failure. With the conscious help of her family she chose to marry a man she did not love, and her husband, in turn, regarded her as an adjunct to his own professional development and constantly berated her for her inability to function well and for her recurrent depressions, in contrast to his own "normality."

I remember well seeing Susan for the first time in consultation. She was regressed, crying, complaining of being depressed, hopeless, unable to cope, unable to bear a child, unfit for anything else, a chronic failure, a disgrace to her family and her husband. I also remember after the session feeling angry and depressed and wondering how I could possibly help her in any way. The history, however, did indicate that her previous analysis had been of significant help in getting her through her reaction to miscarriages and in functioning despite many suicidal fantasies.

It is important to emphasize that Susan put part of her depression and feelings of helplessness into her analyst both during the consultation and in the early stages of her analysis. This process was an externalization of what had been done to her by her family and was now being done by her husband.

Through analysis four times per week, she came to see that the process of projective identification had occurred repeatedly within her nuclear family since childhood. The analyst's reception of her depression was diagnostic of Susan's own internal processes.

Susan came to recognize that she had unconsciously "chosen" her husband so that she could repeat her family role. Similarly, he "chose" her, unconsciously, as a masochistic adjunct into whom he could put his depression and fears in a projective identificatory way. Susan also had a series of female friends to whose problems she listened, absorbed, and was depressed by, while her friends were relieved. Interpretations were directed to the "carrying nature" as well as the "caring nature" of her ego. She learned to distinguish between those depressions reactive to life events from those put into her, especially by her husband.

There were, of course, other factors involved. She needed to fail in her relationship with a man and to subordinate herself to her female friends on an oedipal basis. Her "dumping" of feelings had an anal form. Her oral fixation lead to a swallowing or taking in of the depressive symptoms of others.

She and her husband were intertwined in a relationship where he provided total direction for her life. He would, however, become angry and restrict her food and finances for everyday living, just as her mother had done.

The therapeutic work was quite successful. Susan conceived and bore a child. She was able to separate from her husband and what he was doing to her psychologically. She filed for separation and then divorce. She was able to relate in a more significant way to her family, recognizing how they were using her, and as a consequence, as might be expected, her parents had to learn to deal with their own depression over retirement and approaching old age. Susan was able to help her brother, who entered therapy himself to deal with his emerging depression and repeated failures with women and in his profession. She was no longer the scapegoat, so to speak, for the problems of other people.

During this analytic work, the analyst was repeatedly depressed by Susan. This was not due to any personal problems of his own, but due to her, by what she "did" to him. Susan had been brought up in a family where a large amount of projective identification was the norm. Both she and her family repeatedly depressed others. The analyst, furthermore, was vulnerable because of his therapeutic stance: he attempted to be consciously and unconsciously attuned to his patient. He realized, however, in contrast to his patient, that the depression and depressive fantasies and his counterreactions to the patient, which, presumably, were based on unconscious phantasies and depressive affects projected into him by her, were part of *Susan's* psychological system and not his own. This realization led to instant relief, and also to enlightenment about the dynamics of Susan's relations with others, the process in the therapy being a reflection of what was done to Susan in her everyday life. Susan, too, was helped to recognize in herself what was done to her by others. She saw how she had been brought up to be a readily available container for other people, and learned to recognize her own receptiveness to others' depressive psychic parts.

THE SCAPEGOAT PHENOMENON

From the above it can be seen that certain individuals are selected as scapegoats in families. This is not a new phenomenon. In the case of Susan, a particular individual who was of the "wrong" sex was selected by her family quite unconsciously to carry their failure and depression. The family had an underlying sense of failure and depression about themselves. Further, one can see how Susan responded with the angry provocation of obesity in adolescence, denying that it was a problem, and with determination to get pregnant at all costs. Her family and husband encouraged Susan's responses. She, in turn, was caught up in their manic defenses as their object of contempt for being such a weakling. By identification with them, she had at times a narcissistic sense of omnipotence, which had to be worked on in the treatment. She introjected their depressive projective identifications easily, and had done so since early childhood.

Her depressions were over real or fantasied losses, but these were aggrandized by the family's pouncing upon them, while they minimized their own sense of failure and personal losses within their marriage, friendships, and professional failures. Susan's own angry, depressed sense of futility was also revealed in the analysis. Her tendency to accept the scapegoat role came up again in the social and professional groups to which she belonged. These she learned to deal with quite successfully.

DEPRESSING THE THERAPIST

It is exciting to work with extremely disturbed, schizophrenic, or borderline patients, and therapists as well as theorists find this fascinating work. The understanding that comes from working with such patients in contacting their primitive psychic functioning and forms of primitive defense is valuable. There is a sense of acceptable omnipotence that comes from the understanding and successful treatment of these very difficult patients.

To work with the depressed is not as exciting. The slow, methodical work with the chronically complaining, hypochondrical, and depressed patient is tedious. Even the most psychologically minded therapist must refer severely depressed patients for treatment by organic methods. Thus, the therapist backs away from depression within clinical settings as much as he or she does outside them.

Is it possible that depressed patients with suicidal fantasies and the persecutory aspects of hypochondriasis threaten all of us? We all get depressed, but this truism has resulted in a theoretical homily, a statement that is acknowledged but then dismissed by clinicians. Of course, we all get depressed. How we become depressed by our patients is discussed only rarely.

Charles was a 67-year-old whose career was coming to an end. He was negotiating desperately with his company to allow him to extend his working years in order to provide for himself financially. His wife was a provocative alcoholic. Charles felt a sense of total alienation. All of these factors could be attributed to a childhood psychological pattern extending throughout his life, where he coped by turning to his work. I was reminded by him of the demands of my own profession and conjured up fantasies about my own future.

Sessions with Charles were laborious and depressing, and I found myself wondering where I could dispatch him or dump him. I needed to work on my own reactions to him, on the sense of burden that he was "inflicting" on me, on my anger at the colleague who had made the referral and at myself for having taken him on.

What was his life about? Charles was depressing and he depressed me. At first I preferred to ignore this, with the usual therapists' rationalizations about the need for empathy in the therapeutic situation. Charles, however, also evoked in me questions about the meaning of my own professional life, a life that would parallel his at times, and anxiety about what was in store for me on retirement (fortunately some years away). The patient seemed better after the sessions but I was much worse. I began to understand that he was putting part of his depression into me, as a container for it, and I was becoming afraid of being overwhelmed.

Characteristically, my original defenses were a denial of this, accompanied by omnipotent fantasies about what I could do for him, and, for that matter, for myself. I resorted to the manic defenses described so well by the Kleinian school (Segal 1973), developed a feeling of contempt for Charles, and came to feel that I could control the situation and triumph in an omnipotent way because my capabilities were greater than his. Even a falling out of the therapeutic role into a directive form of therapy was of no help to Charles.

As I was working hard to deal with Charles I came to understand how other people reacted to him. They avoided him as much as I did. His wife talked of divorce; his daughters distanced themselves from him. I, too, wished to find some way of "divorcing" and dumping him into another therapeutic institution.

Recognition is, of course, the first step in reversing a reaction. I realized that Charles need not depress me, nor did I need to use my ineffectual defensive coping patterns. One does not have to be overwhelmed by a patient's projective identifications. Showing Charles what he did to his wife and others was helpful to him. Among other things it helped him to negotiate an extension of his contract at work. This, too, lessened his depressive effect upon others, who no longer backed away from him in an angry, depressed way. He was able to persuade his wife to seek help for her alcoholism. She stopped threatening to divorce him, which in turn eased the pressure upon him.

This is not to diminish the problem of dealing with the psychology of Charles's old age. Yet it illustrates very clearly how patients such as Charles stir up in us anxieties about our professional lives, and our own fantasies about aging and mortality, fantasies that we deny. Patients like Charles, of course, prompt us to think of our own death.

In cases such as Charles's the therapist is vulnerable. Part of this is due to the therapeutic stance that renders the therapist susceptible to the patient's projections. Others outside the therapeutic situation are less at risk in that when they cannot tolerate the depression, they can resist an attempt to embroil them by avoidance by walking away. Usually this is not possible in therapeutic situations, except when there has been a rupture in the therapeutic relationship. Nevertheless, at times therapists will attempt to retreat psychologically from depressed patients while they are apparently involved in the therapy.

Another aspect of the vulnerability of the therapist is that the therapeutic boundaries, which are psychological, may be more permeable in therapeutic situations, particularly with certain patients with whom certain therapists will identify. I was, perhaps, more vulnerable to Charles because of my coping attempts to deal with my anger at having to treat him. To overcompensate for this anger I became overly involved in his personal life, as I have described. In addition, my empathy turned to sympathy because I related his difficulties at work to the increasing demands of my own professional life, and to my own concerns about aging and the future.

Thus, while our personalities had little in common, some of the processes in our lives were sufficiently similar to resonate within me and cause a temporary rupture of the psychological boundaries between us, so that the patient's depression depressed me. The recognition of this boundary problem helped me, as did my reminder to myself that the depressive content and fantasies, which Charles had, belonged to him and not to me.

THE CREATOR OF DEPRESSION

While we deal routinely with patients who are depressed for various reasons we hear indirectly about people who make them so. On occasion we have patients who are the instigators of depression by projective identification in others.

> Collin, a 45-year-old senior executive, was referred to me after he was given my name by his ex-wife, who was in psychotherapy with a colleague for suicidal and depressive behavior, apparently precipitated by the breakup of their marriage two years earlier. The precipitating event in Collin's case, however, was, on the surface, a second severe loss of job status.
>
> The first had occurred four years before he came to me, when he learned to his horror that he had been passed over for a very senior position in an industrial corporation. The bad news, which was a severe blow to his narcissism, came not

directly but in the morning newspaper. His wife, Ellen, was very supportive at that time. Competent and socially well connected, Collin was able to move to another firm, where the same pattern repeated itself. Difficulties with very senior executives represented a hidden, unresolved oedipal problem.

By the time he arrived for analysis, Collin was in the process of final negotiations for a position, on a contractual basis, with a high salary, and for severance pay. He had left his wife because of her alleged neurotic difficulties, which he claimed had been aggravated by his rise to success.

Analytic work dictated that we had to look at Collin's identifications with his father and mother, who were extremely successful people, the former a businessman, the latter a socialite. They were, so to speak, without any psychological problems. One suspects that they projected their own failures and difficulties into particular members of their own respective families as each one seemed to have a "casualty" in it.

The patient was unable to compete directly with his father, but they worked in related fields. Collin functioned well under his father's tutelage, but difficulties began to arise due to Collin's underlying dislike of authority. Within the family atmosphere, failure was never allowed. Even a bout of tuberculosis in late adolescence, which almost ruined his academic career, was handled in the family with an almost "manic" collusion, extolling the benefits of such an illness. True to form, he read extensively and argued that his euphoria at the time was due only to the tubercular infection.

Collin had married Ellen twelve years before I met him, and they had three children. He complained about her constant preoccupation with social climbing and about her scheming and maneuvering to aid him. At the same time he complained that when he met her she was an unsuccessful executive in the same company as he, and he believed she had been having an affair with his superior. This caused him no end of chagrin in his fantasies and feelings about her, but he triumphed in his conquest of her and won her away from his oedipal rival in the firm. Their marriage was not a happy one. Collin blamed Ellen entirely for this, and said that she had entered into marriage with him only as a way to avoid facing her failure to climb the corporate ladder.

The marriage was stormy. Collin described himself as quite normal, despite having repeated affairs. Ellen found out about some of these and raised a furor. She complained constantly about his derisory ways and about the way in which he undercut her whenever she made efforts within the community women's associations. They seemed to be caught up in a masochistic–sadistic relationship. Although separated, they could not stay apart from each other since they were hurt and hurting constantly.

It is easy to see the possibility that Ellen was, in fact, the depressive carrier for the failure of this hitherto "normal" man. He attributed his work failures to her and she became depressed over this. She had been a deprived child and in her adult years rejection led to feelings of deprivation and intense depression. Collin was not much help. Ellen would feel suicidal when he suffered a setback. She dreaded constantly that she would be deserted by him. She had been deserted by her father, and Collin deserted her by having affairs. Collin, on the other hand, suffered only temporary feelings of depression in his business setbacks. Even the major one, four years earlier, led to more anguish in Collin's wife. The current setback was the first time that Collin had really experienced depression. He had rationalized even the marital breakup, two years previously, as being due to his wife's severe character disorder.

The therapeutic work went well at first because Collin regarded both of us as superior men who had to manage as executives in a difficult world. Soon interpretations about how he unconsciously used Ellen began to take effect, and the patient became very depressed. We reviewed his life, and he experienced the depressions he had not experienced before. These included the concealed reaction to his adolescent illness and his hitherto denied depressions over certain academic failures, some of which had been glossed over (his not getting a higher degree, for example), and his grief over the breakup of his marriage.

He had used his wife as a container for his own failures, and got her to worry about his future. As might be expected, he tended to put some of this into me, and I began to wonder about him, too. Because I recognized what was going on, I could convey to the patient what he was doing to me and what he had done to Ellen.

A casualty developed in the form of his elder son, who became a school dropout and, in turn, entered treatment for depression. The son's depression was labeled by his therapist as a depression over the loss of his parents, through the marriage breakup. It was alleviated to a certain extent by the reunion of his parents, who benefited from their treatment so much that they reunited permanently. A follow-up interview three years later suggested a good marital readjustment, with the partners each taking responsibility for their own psychological problems. Ellen did not return to the business world but was reported to function well as a person in her own right.

THE THERAPIST WHO DEPRESSES OTHERS

One of the most important reasons for therapists or analysts to undergo personal therapy or analysis is to be helped to discern the problems from their own childhoods that they carry into adulthood and bring to their therapeutic work. They must be aware of these problems so that they will not take them out on their patients or clients. It may well be that some "wounded healers," being seen in treatment by their colleagues, at times may be barely able to function in their private lives. The crucial point, however, is not how healthy or sick they may be at any given time but that their "wounds" do not adversely affect their patients. The chronically depressed therapist has to be aware of any tendency he or she might have to make his or her patients depressed.

James was a respected psychiatrist with a large psychotherapy practice. His analysis revealed that he had experienced a great deal of maternal and paternal deprivation. His depressed and angry mother rejected both James and his younger sister, periodically, when they were children. She was verbally abusive to him and berated him about his alleged shortcomings. He often felt humiliated and was, internally, very resentful.

Although on the surface James was a gentle and responsible physician, much of these qualities was due to reaction formations to his internal feelings of depression and anger. Unconsciously he identified with his mother, and unconsciously he turned many of his patients into depressive casualties by focusing almost exclusively upon the depressive aspects of their narratives while totally ignoring the "goodness" or functioning aspects of their egos and superegos. James seemed to forget that the latter has a facilitating and directive function as well as a critical one. From his interaction with his mother and father, James had developed an internal superego that was not enabling. Similarly, he could not enable his patients, but without being aware that he did so, undermined them so that they became depressed.

Some of James's patients apprehended this. His own depressive symptomatology was readily apparent and they would ask him how he felt. James would reply to these enquiries, tell the patient about his migraine headaches, and so forth. It did not seem to occur to him that this kind of response, rather than interpretations about the underlying nature of the enquiry, was not helping the patient at all.

When James overcame his own problems, he realized that his patients' anxious enquiries about his mental health and his headaches were prompted by unconscious phantasies and conscious fantasies that they had harmed him. Some of his replies to these queries, such as "It's just one of those days," had not helped those who came to him for treatments; they had depressed them further. James then had had to deal with more deeply depressed patients and himself became even more depressed.

James is an example of a therapist who is vulnerable as a result of his own upbringing. Indeed, in James's case, this vulnerability created a need in him to depress his own children, who were, in turn, chronically depressed. While his remarks to his patients appear on the surface to be innocent ones, analytic scrutiny reveals them to be cover-ups for quite aggressive responses, and for James's fantasies that the patients were burdens upon him. James had come to realize that his mother had felt, perhaps, that he and his sister were burdens upon her. Since she intervened in his life repeatedly, as his father did not, James identified with her as the stronger parent in the family. Thus James's intervention in his patients' lives was not of a helpful nature, as his mother's had not been in his. While not verbally abusive to his patients, largely by focusing almost exclusively upon the miserable and depressing aspects of their lives, James put them into a depressed and dependent position. He ignored the phenomenon of "splitting"—that the patients put good aspects of their lives into other people for safekeeping, and that these represented good objects in contrast to the bad objects (all representing internal splits between good and bad objects)—and that many of his own good feelings were by projective identification put into other people, whom he then enhanced by regarding them as good, idealized, and so on. This process emptied him even further, psychologically, and depressed him about himself even more. Beneath his calm manner, in his transactions with his patients, James also indulged in subtle nonverbal maneuvers—wearing a pained facial expression when he had a headache, for example—which also depressed them and put them down, as his mother, in a more forceful and open way, had depressed and put him down.

Other depressed therapists may have to look at situations in their own childhoods similar to those that James experienced, where what was done to them happened in more covert ways. We should, too, acknowledge the validity of the criticism that sometimes therapists are casualties who have gone into the therapeutic professions in an endeavor to deal with their own internal problems. These problems may include depressions. It is, however, possible by personal therapy or analysis to see what one does, or might do, to one's patients or clients and overcome the need to create as external objects (representing internal objects) particular relationships from one's early childhood in the treatment of others, in transference to the patient.

THE DEPRESSED CLINICAL TEAM

As we have said, depressed patients are depressing. They depress not only the therapist but those in the treatment unit as well. This is usually dealt with in the all-important team conference where reactions to the patient are aired.

Quite often at these meetings staff will adopt a derisory attitude toward certain depressed patients. They will express wry amusement at the patient's apparent difficulty in coping with the loss of objects, and at the entanglement of his or her personal relationships, relationships in which the patient engineers rejection. This is a defense against the internal, personal, and private difficulties that the patient has stirred up in the nursing staff, support staff, and the therapist. Each member of the staff may attempt to cope with this private turmoil and depression privately, but it is important to consider how depressed individuals can depress the whole clinical team.

Clinical case conferences and team conferences are psychodynamic small groups and can be depressed by discussion of particular patients. The effects of small-group dynamics upon therapists and patients will be elaborated in the following chapter. We have to recognize, however, that depressed patients, particularly the more severely depressed, can evoke similar responses in those individuals who care for them, just as psychotic patients can make a team "psychotic" for periods of time. This is due in part to identification with the patient, but it may also be a result of introjection of the patient's projective identification of depressive parts. Being cared for by depressed staff depresses the depressed patient still further, even when the patient has originated the situation. Recognition by staff of the projective identification system can halt the process rapidly.

It must also be recognized that a depressed clinical team carries the depression that has been evoked into its case discussions and dealings with other patients. Dealing with a number of deeply depressed psychotic and clinically depressed individuals as patients has a profound effect on those who care for them. If this is unacknowledged in the teamwork and team conferences the effect will increase. A whole ward staff can become overwhelmed by its work, and patients who have been admitted for other reasons in turn may be unconsciously and unintentionally depressed by the staff, who have been depressed by others.

CARRYOVER

Barbara, a child therapist in personal analysis, reported a case she observed through a one-way screen.

One of her colleagues was treating a 5-year-old child whose father had died in an automobile accident when the child was 1 year old. Both the mother and child were seen, sometimes together and sometimes separately. Those who observed behind the screen constituted a psychological small group.

It soon became clear to both the therapist and those watching that a "heavy trip" had been placed upon the 5 year-old boy. He had to deal with his unconscious phantasy that he had in some way caused his father's death. This was not true in actuality, of course, but was part of his unconscious phantasy system. Here, at the height of his oedipal phase, he had to deal with his phantasy that he had unconsciously killed his father and thereby had his mother all to himself. In addition, his mother and others who knew them saw in him the survivor and successor to his father, to be responsible for continuing the family name.

Barbara reported a particular session with great turmoil in her own analysis. The child was running about the room, and the therapist and the mother, who was present, began to talk about his apparently "manic" behavior, which also took place at home and in kindergarten. When touchy material about his father's death came into the discussions between the therapist and the mother, the child ran about the playroom in a destructive and self-destructive way. The therapist asked the mother what she thought she should do in order to help her son. The mother, who had previously said she was baffled, came up with the response that perhaps she should hold him, though he had often shrugged off such a thing. She held out her arms to her son, who came running toward her, and she held her son in her arms and he cried. The therapist also cried at this point; and Barbara, who was behind the one-way screen, cried as well.

In the discussion afterward, everyone behind the screen had uncontrollable sadness. This carried on in each of them, they reported, into the rest of the day.

Subsequently, Barbara was quite dysfunctional in her own analytic session. She was, so to speak, verbalizing "all over the lot," unable to focus, just as the child she had observed was unable to focus. She spoke of her own fantasies, which came from her unconscious phantasies that she had destroyed others in her own relationships.

The depressing effects of this one session with the child carried into the rest of Barbara's work in the next few days. Much solace had to be given, also, to the child's therapist.

Fortunately, the child's phantasies that he had destroyed his father came out of his verbal discussion with the therapist, as his mother held him, in his following session.

Barbara, as a result of insight gained in her own analytic sessions, was able to deal openly with severely depressing issues in the lives of her patients, which she had not been able to confront in the previous six days between the sessions observed through the one-way screen. She was also able to relate directly to issues concerning her own hidden violent phantasies toward others in her life.

Here we see how a clinical case, in this case that of a depressed child and mother, may have profound effects upon a therapist and upon a psychological small group (the clinical team who observed behind the one-way screen), effects that last for hours and days. The child displayed his depression by hyperactive behavior, loosely termed "manic" by Barbara. The mother handled hers by self-control and denial and a regressive inability, initially, to think how to deal constructively with the aggressive and self-destructive behavior of her child, whose running about even in the playroom resulted in bumping, spilling, and accidents, which hurt him in minor ways but were probably symbolic of his way of handling his guilt over his imagined destruction of his father. Some of this was probably also oedipal guilt over having his mother to himself.

Massive depressive affects *are* created by clinically depressed patients. The small group observing this case were fortunate in that, because of the clinical setting, they were able to talk about the depression that had been stirred up in each one of them by watching the sessions and relating them to their personal life histories. The insight gained as a result of his session, nevertheless, was of enormous value to the patient, to his mother, to the therapist, and to the clinical team. It freed Barbara to work in her own analysis with aspects of her life she had had trouble seeing, her depression and—hitherto less acceptable to her—the violence of her aggressive, unconscious phantasies, and, later, conscious fantasies about her failed relationships.

THE DISGUISED DEPRESSION

Chronic fatigue, insomnia, and hypochondriacal preoccupation suggest manifestations of a depressive pattern or the way in which a particular individual expresses the underlying psychodynamics of his own personality and life circumstances. These disguised depressive aspects can also be projected. Also, the persecutory aspects of such hypochondriasis (Rosenfeld 1965) can be detected in the recipient, for example in the therapist, into whom these projections are made and introjected.

Louise, a 35-year-old married woman in therapy, was preoccupied with bodily complaints, which throughout her life had resulted in multiple visits to her family practitioner for a variety of reasons. She had been given a large number of medical and surgical remedies. She complained of chronic fatigue and pestered for pills as oral gratification to alleviate her symptoms. Her clinging behavior had disturbed members of the general and surgical units on a number of her admissions and had ultimately led to a psychiatric referral.

It is interesting that her hypochondriasis was noted to stir up similar symptomatology in a number of the nursing staff. In the course of her therapy, her therapist observed that he also became preoccupied with his health. Louise's symptoms reflected a sophisticated knowledge of various medical conditions. The therapist began to worry about his own health until he recognized that Louise was evoking in him, in his countertransference, similar fantasies to her own, and preoccupations about cancer and heart disease, fantasies that were particularly intense during psychotherapy sessions with her. Recognition of the therapeutic reactions led to an alleviation of the therapist's anxiety, since then he could focus on Louise's actions and the chronic tormenting aspects of her psychosomatic symptomatology.

As Louise was involved in a number of hospitalizations for investigation during the early part of the therapy, part of the case management meant the use of an intermediary psychiatric consultant to convey to the medical and surgical teams some of the aspects of what she evoked in those around her, including how she handled her depression. The consultant emphasized the way in which Louise handled depression in terms of making others depressed and arousing fatigue and hypochondriacal worries in nursing and support staff.

Disguised depressions in therapists and staff can be diagnosed by the recognition and open admission of the fantasies that are stirred up by the patient, in treatment or in clinical case conference. Questions such as how the therapist, support staff, and nursing staff *feel* about the patient, what fantasies they have, and what these mean in relation to the patient are of crucial importance. All patients and clients stir up fantasies and unconscious phantasies, but it is possible for therapists and support staff to monitor regularly what is going on in their fantasy systems, which are within their egos, in the ongoing process of psychotherapy and patient care. It is these fantasies, which are stirred up, that are diagnostic and that help make process interpretations and confrontations to patients. In the case of Louise, her hypochondriasis produced similar symptomatology in the staff and the therapist who looked after her. The recognition by the therapist that these had been "put into him" and into the nursing staff was diagnostic. Similar fantasies were evoked in the medical and surgical teams, and a diagnosis was made that Louise's hypochondriasis and fatigue were, in fact, the ways in which she handled depression. What was projected were phantasies that stirred up conscious fantasies. It was not easy for the staff to admit to open depression and there was enough concern about their own anxiety about personal illness. What was projected was, all-in-all, disguised depression. A review of Louise's case confirmed that she had, indeed, the classical symptoms of a disguised depression. She was treated by antidepressants and supportive psychotherapy, and support from her physicians, surgeons, and nursing staff.

The case conference can be of great benefit in the diagnosis and treatment of such patients as Louise, provided the participants are functioning as a Work Group (we shall come to more discussion of group psychodynamics), provided that they are a group, that is, that is focused on the task and is not overly infused by other nonwork activities. Such a group can examine the feelings and fantasies that the case arouses in the therapist who is presenting and in themselves.

WHAT KINDS OF DEPRESSION ARE INVOLVED?

In an earlier chapter, depression was discussed from a number of etiological bases. Here the focus is upon how others, including therapists and support staff, are made depressed by patients.

Again, Fairbairn (1952) and Guntrip (1961, 1968) discuss the schizoid sense of futility, which at first seems similar to, but which is distinguished from, depression. The sufferer is unable to relate to an internal object. He or she projects representations of this onto an external object or person, then feels a sense of futility about his or her inability to relate to this other person or to others. This state is usually chronic and is often confused with chronic depression. It may also turn up in the "phenotypes" of chronic depression in epidemiological studies of depression in various populations. The results in treating these patients by antidepressant therapy are not very good, and the therapist's lack of success is regarded by the patient as one more thing that, like everything else in his or her life, was doomed to fail.

Patients who suffer from a constant inability to relate to people make up a large proportion of long-term psychotherapy and psychoanalytic cases. They often evoke a sense of futility in therapists about their own life and life in general. The whole question of existential anxiety comes into therapeutic focus. Even the most well-adjusted therapist will be disturbed by questions about the patient's real nature, ways of existence, and the meaning of life. Such sessions are painful for both therapist and patient. It is, of course, the prerogative of both patient and therapist to look at the meaning of life, a task performed by the patient both in and out of sessions, and by the therapist away from the therapeutic setting. Most of us can function, recognizing the limitations and difficulties of interpersonal relationships that reflect some of the difficulties of our internal worlds; we then bring the internal world into our relationships in the external. Life, for most of us, has great meaning.

The most common form of reactive depression or neurotic depression stems from feelings of rejection. It results from an inability to deal with the anger this rejection, real or imagined, arouses. The ambivalently loved lost object is introjected in an identificatory way and internally attacked. Chronic depression over repeated rejections, or fantasied rejections or anticipated rejection, may look very similar to a chronic sense of futility. In these cases patients repeatedly put themselves into situations in which they get others to reject them.

Depression as a result of guilt is also commonplace, though experience shows that such patients are more likely to keep the depression as an internal problem, letting their superegos torment them for what they have done, whether real or imagined. There is usually less of this form of depression put into other people, since it is usually important for the patient to maintain an internal sense of suffering and guilt. Those, however, who have been raised on the basis of guilt, at

times, unconsciously, may use this mode of relating to others
and thereby depress the therapist.

Mary was a 36-year-old divorcee, a single-parent
mother of two children. Her custody of the children had
survived several legal battles. Her husband, whom she described as sadistic, used his family's connections to instigate
various legal maneuvres to challenge the custody, and had
succeeded in severely restricting her alimony.

Mary had had a religious upbringing. She, with her
siblings, had been brought up in a friendly but emphatically
moral environment. She identified strongly with this, and was
prone to moralize about others' behavior, particularly that of
her former husband. Her strong principles had been a source
of strength to her at difficult times in her life. They gave her a
cohesive sense of self. Sometimes, however, these self-
reflections were extreme: she fell into self-moralizing and was
also very critical of others. She had few friends to help alleviate
her loneliness and only slowly, in therapy, came to understand
that her censorious attitude and her repeated personal feelings
of guilt made others back away.

As a patient, too, she moralized about the therapeutic
work. Periods of tension in the transference led her to leave the
treatment room loudly reprimanding the therapist, in a high-
pitched voice, for his ineptitude and inability to maintain a
facilitating therapeutic environment. Interpretations were regarded as attacks, and Mary would leap up and leave the
session, slamming doors. She was a tormented woman.

Mary, unconsciously too, had seemed to find a man to
marry who would torment her—and, indeed, he did, both
during the marriage and by means of the legal wrangles concerning her support, the custody of the children, and so on,
when the marriage was over. Unconsciously she felt herself to
be a guilty person. She had many phantasies about what she
had done in the marriage and how she had affected various
other people. This chronic sense of guilt took the form of
depressive symptomatology. In the therapy Mary uncon-

sciously attempted to manipulate the therapist into forming a similar object relationship where he was the tormentor. When he adopted a neutral stance she felt that he was being difficult and unhelpful to her. Her remarks were an unintentional attempt to make him feel guilty for his alleged maltreatment. Then, faced with an imagined rejecting and maltreating therapist, she would storm out of the room, leaving the therapist behind to wonder what he had done wrong, and to feel guilty and depressed.

On reflection the therapist observed that on many occasions in the treatment of Mary he had felt guilty and depressed. Mary had, by projective identification, put her guilty depression into him. He did not *have* to feel guilty about his interpretations. As well as being of considerable relief, this realization illuminated, and helped him show to Mary, how she made those around her feel they "walked on eggs," and how this mode of relating had developed in childhood in her religious and moralistic family. The therapist did not need to have an internal sense of suffering and torment about his imaginary wrongdoings as he had done nothing wrong. Mary's self-tormenting guilt was *her* problem and not his.

Therapists see a wide spectrum of depressions in the course of their work and it is easy for them to introject some of them unwittingly and then attempt to deal with their own depression without recognizing from whence it has come. To deny that the patient is evoking feelings and fantasies in oneself is, in itself, diagnostic. Manic defenses of triumph, control, derision of the patient, and omnipotence about the therapeutic work on the part of the therapist may be valuable diagnostic signs of what is happening in the patient.

THERAPIST VARIABLES

Are certain therapists more vulnerable to being affected or even overwhelmed by depressing patients? Under what circumstances are therapists vulnerable?

Obviously, a range of therapeutic personalities deals with a range of patients who, in turn, express a range of variables. The extent to which one is affected by a particular patient depends on a variety of circumstances (including the results of one's personal therapy or analysis) in the patient's life or in one's own.

In the analysis of a professional, Arthur, who was himself practicing marital therapy, we had to work with the depressing aspects of his own potential marriage breakup, how he came to be married to a particular woman, and how they interrelated and how they did not. Arthur could not, of course, suspend his professional life until he had worked out a solution to his own external and internal problems but had to continue working in his hospital and private practice.

Much of Arthur's professional work resonated with his own problems. The marital couples he dealt with were struggling with problems, and often overwhelmed by feelings about them. Some of these problems struck areas within his own internal world, which further depressed him. Sometimes Arthur would come to his sessions and report his own therapeutic work: he dealt with deeply depressed people who made him more depressed but seemed better themselves after sessions with him. This process seemed to involve the mechanisms discussed, and part of our analytic work dealt with Arthur's introjection of others' depressions. We worked, therefore, with aspects of Arthur's life related to his childhood, his current situation, and with those elements that were "put into him" by his patients.

Sometimes he was involved in long-term psychotherapy with patients who had life histories very similar to his own: ambitious, hard-driving professionals, with immigrant parents with great expectations for their sons. We worked on his intolerance of his own failures and the failures of others, and his close identification with certain patients. At times, he lived part of his life vicariously through them. Blows to their narcissism became blows to his. In his projective identification, Arthur almost literally put himself into particular patients.

Arthur's therapeutic vulnerability was not constant. With the resolution of his own marital difficulties, Arthur became more tolerant of the difficulties of others and less affected and depressed by them. His personal analysis, by examining and working on his narcissistic vulnerability and his overidentification with some others, led to a lessening of the overinvolvement with certain patients and, therefore, a lessening of his vulnerability to the depressive aspects of their lives.

Social variables are important. The therapist who is unable to talk about the cases that depress him feels isolated and is therefore probably more vulnerable. While patient confidentiality is of paramount importance, most therapists benefit from talking in disguised ways to someone about their patients, and since most therapists need to unwind at the end of the day, they often chat with their partners about their work. Provided individual confidentiality is not at risk, they should not feel bad about this—although stern lectures by other therapists, analysts, and supervisors may be intended to induce feelings of guilt about what is normal, and probably necessary, behavior (this is not to advocate depressing the partner by unloading the depression into him or her, of course).

Some therapists have reported that they lighten the burden of depressive work by taking on other patients to whom they can relate as "partners." This is *not* a useful way of dealing with the psychological load of everyday work. What is most helpful to therapists is to realize that the fantasies, feelings, and phantasies (unconscious) put into them by patients belong to the patients and not to themselves, though they may well be useful and, indeed, may well stir up what is part and parcel of the therapist's own experience. The "over-

load phenomenon" can best be relieved by developing a sense
of what is one's own and what is not. To return to the case of
Mary described above: Mary worried constantly about what
she was doing wrong in her life. At times she made her
therapist worry in the same way. When she left her sessions
early, slamming doors, he felt guilty and depressed, and reflected upon what he had said that might have upset her so.
When he recognized that he was the recipient of massive
projections of Mary's guilt and depression, then he could
reverse the effect.

DISRUPTED EQUILIBRIUM

A therapist's functioning can be destabilized by changes in the
behavior of others toward him or her.

> Roger, a middle-aged therapist, experienced a marriage
> breakup when his hitherto rather dependent wife, Helen, as a
> result of her own analysis, decided to terminate the marriage.
> Helen expressed a great deal of anger toward Roger. She
> moved among her friends, including Roger's colleagues and
> their partners, voicing her discontent with him and talking
> about her former masochistic compliance with his forceful and
> domineering ways. She evoked much sympathy, particularly
> from female friends and from Roger's professional colleagues'
> wives. As a result of Helen's leaving him, Roger became
> visibly depressed.
> He did not stop his therapeutic or teaching work, of
> course, but carried on as before. He was reported to be rather
> "strained" and depressed in some seminars he gave, at other
> times flippant or "manic" in some of his remarks to colleagues
> or trainees.
> In his personal life he indulged in a number of fleeting
> affairs with a variety of young women. One of his colleagues
> remarked to him that he seemed to be depressed and depleted

by his separation from his wife, and perhaps he was seeking to restore himself by "feeding" on women. Or did he hope to regain lost youth?

These remarks struck Roger in the conflict-free sphere of his ego and resonated in his internal world. He began to look at what he was doing. He ended his series of transitory affairs and established a stable relationship with a woman of his own age. After a period of depression, and the mourning of his first marriage had been worked through—a working through that was assisted by talking to his peers, his new partner, and by a return to personal analysis—the two moved in together.

Roger's acting out with other women had an effect on other patients in the broader community, and had to be taken up in their therapies and analyses by other therapists and analysts: Were their own therapists equally vulnerable? Were their therapists' marriages intact? Were their therapists and analysts depressed? Were they themselves participants in therapeutic work or would they be used for sexual and depressive acting out?

VULNERABILITY AND EMPATHY

Empathy is part of one's humanity and understanding, and is different from sympathy. In a therapeutic situation empathy is necessary for understanding; sympathy leads to overidentification and overinvolvement. All of us are, nevertheless, vulnerable to the processes described in this and other chapters. In order to be effective the therapist must be attentive, empathetic, sensitive, attuned, open, and therefore vulnerable. At the same time he or she must remain an individual, distinct. The therapist should receive the patients' projective identifications in an ego-functioning way as a receiving psychological container, part of the ego, while not letting these introjects overwhelm him or her internally. The psychic parts belong to the patient. The recognition that they are part of the patient, not the therapist, is crucial.

The catastrophes and horrors in which patients get caught up and live through belong to them, too, even though they may remind us of our own experiences. Patients "do things" to us, but we recognize that it is *their* "doing," by our self-scrutiny and self-analysis as part of our ongoing evaluation and analysis of the counterreaction to the patient.

PROBLEMS WITH SELF PSYCHOLOGY

Regardless of whatever theoretical or conceptual scheme the therapist uses, the therapist is the recipient of what the patient infuses or implodes. This, in my view, is the essence of "therapeutic listening." Guntrip (1960), again, observes that as therapists, we often tolerate badly what he terms "ego weakness," the helpless, dependent part of ourselves, covered by layers of ego and ego defenses, always denied, never recognized, which, in turn, we despise in others, including our patients. This term "ego weakness," a metaphor, is a useful one. Guntrip asserts that most of us prefer "the mighty instincts," particularly about aggressiveness, to the helplessness we sometimes feel about ourselves, particularly in our therapeutic work. We prefer to feel tough and aggressive and, indeed, prefer these qualities in the patients and clients we see before us. Depression in ourselves and others, therefore, is a threat. We prefer our formulations about internally directed hostility about lost objects to those about how we experience losses that threaten our omnipotent defenses, our control of others, and our control of ourselves. We prefer formulations about loss and anger to those about a fundamental inability to relate.

In the same way we prefer our patients to have mastery of their own lives. When patients cannot cope, we feel inner urges to rescue them and render them whole. We may push them, consciously or unconsciously, to regain the sense of self and thereby overcome their vulnerability—and ours. By identification with their aggressiveness, which we ourselves may have aroused, we hope to overcome our own sense of vulnerability as well. This may be the root of some of the appeal function that some writers (Olinick 1980) have referred to. I believe that only certain types of reactive depressions appeal to certain types of therapists because of the resonance within their own personal lives, or because the depressive symptoms are really about shame—the affect that self psychologists believe is the result of a ruptured sense of self, showing defects in mirroring by external objects. It is possible that self psychology itself may be appealing to many because it tends to focus upon what ruptures have occurred in the self by lack of mirroring of narcissistic self objects, rather than upon a basic ego weakness and sense of futility. The latter can be overcome in a transitory way by a restabilization of the sense of self by mirroring. The emphasis, however, is upon self-objects in the external environment of the patient. This detracts from scrutiny of the internal world and the patient's inability to dialogue with internal objects, as represented by external objects. It is this inability that leads to the affect of futility. The subsequent shame about the inability to cope with one's self is secondary. This overemphasis upon mirroring, at times in clinical work, may be a limitation of a self psychology. In my view, the focus is sometimes too much upon the functions of the therapist and not upon the internal world of the patient. The current vogue for hunting for ruptures in the self and for seeing the loss of self-objects in a patient's life may itself be a defensive shift in focus, a shift that has led to criticism of the concept of the self-object as leading all too easily to replacement-object therapy. The approach may lead to the creation of a false-self resolution and away from scrutiny of the internal world and the internal object relations therein. The latter can be intense and painful, and cause one to confront one's own existential anxiety.

Francine was a 30-year-old, well-tailored, college-educated, highly intelligent, charming woman who, seemingly through no fault of her own, kept losing jobs for which she was well qualified and well trained. She was one of a large family, in which the love available was rationed. Her mother had married a man, upon whom she was extremely dependent, largely for his social position and potential future, and strongly urged her daughters to do the same. The mother, perhaps to enhance her own sense of self, had several babies to whom she could relate, though she could not relate to children.

Francine suffered from ruptures in her sense of self. She described her self-fragmentation, feelings of unreality, and sense of lack of inner cohesiveness and harmony. She often unconsciously got others to reassure her. Her therapist found that he was responding to her emotional appeals by reminding her of her intelligence, her capacity, her insight, and so on. All of this "stroking" made her feel better. How ruptures occurred in her narcissistic sense of self, and her self-object needs, also came under scrutiny and led to a temporary enhancement of her self and more success at work.

Underlying this was a deeper sense of self or ego weakness, which was very frightening to her and, at first, to her therapist. Francine was unable to form relationships. She feared that she, or her love, would damage her external objects (representing internal objects) and was unable, therefore, to relate to her sexual partners and others in her personal relationships except in temporary ways. Francine caused her friends, her lovers and, indeed, her therapist to search for reasons why things had gone wrong. This caused her to feel shame about herself as a person, and this shame manifested itself in what resembled a depressive state. Her therapist coped with the sense of vulnerability she evoked, and also projected, in himself by focusing on what exactly had occurred to cause such ruptures in her, and where they had occurred in her childhood. He had more difficulty with her basic feeling of emptiness, which began to show up in the therapy and was linked to her very early childhood.

It seemed most likely that Francine's mother had used babies as narcissistic self-objects to handle her own fragmented sense of self. Francine in her therapeutic work had to look not only at ruptures in her own sense of self but at the way in which she unconsciously got others to form self-objects or to seek these for her. What was, however, more frightening to her was her underlying inability to have any relationships, except in the most transitory way. Beneath her loss of sense of self and loss of harmony was a fundamental sense of futility, and the fear that she would destroy anyone she loved with whom she became involved. She had the unconscious phantasy that she had driven away her mother and that the mother had, therefore, had another baby, thus furthering the abandonment process. Francine had developed a charming, appealing personality, a false-self (Winnicott) so that she would be liked and never abandoned again. The fundamental therapeutic work which had to be done was in the face of the "awful chasm" that opened before both Francine and her therapist as they saw the utter sense of futility she had within her. Reassurance, and her finding of transient replacement objects—even the therapist as replacement object—would be of only temporary avail.

SUICIDE

Sometimes depressed patients kill themselves: so do depressed therapists sometimes.

It was Freud (1920) who first proposed that in the suicidal patient it is the aggressive energy that in reality, is unconsciously directed against another person that is turned against oneself. Stengel (1964) says that suicide is murder in reverse. He differentiates between those who kill themselves and those who make suicidal attempts as being in two categories that overlap.

Buckman (1985) suggests we should recognize, not minimize, our difficulties in dealing with suicidal patients. These patients provoke in therapists the same negative and bizarre responses that they provoke in their own families, friends, and peers. Hostility and death wishes from those close to the patient lend to the act (Rosenbaum and Richman 1970).

Some therapists are unwilling to recognize the seriousness of suicidal communication. In some the suicidal patient may produce feelings of malice and aversion, and a hostile countertransference, which may be a major obstacle to treatment (Buckman 1985). A similar hostility by therapists is felt toward patients who chronically self-inflict wounds. These behaviors threaten any omnipotent fantasies therapists may have, particularly if the patient has convinced the therapist that only he or she can help. The therapist is then unanswerably positioned to feel worthless, and to become hostile to the patient for his or her rejection of the therapist's rescue.

THE THERAPIST'S SUICIDE

The incidence of suicide among mental health professionals is high. This suggests either that those who enter the mental health professions are from a particularly vulnerable sample of the population, or that the peculiar stresses of the work make those who perform it vulnerable. The work is, indeed, stressful.

The suicide of a therapist leads to phantasies of responsibility for the death, by unconscious phantasies, in a patient, even as conscious fantasies and a sense of abandonment result from the death. It is important that the patient resume therapy so that he or she can deal with the feelings of imagined implication, guilt over imagined destructive impulses and hostility, and with the fantasy that the new therapist will likewise commit suicide. This last is a displacement of the murderous phantasies toward the predecessor.

TO SUM UP

That depressive patients are depressed and depressing, while common knowledge, is minimized in the literature on the supervision and training of psychotherapists. The therapist, in his therapeutic role, is vulnerable to the patient's depression because he or she is attuned to what the patient is saying in both conscious and unconscious ways.

Depression, particularly on the basis of real or phantasied object loss, is not a "respectable" illness. Threats to self-esteem, and the ensuing shame, and threats to the ego ideal also lead to depressive symptoms.

Depressed patients put their depression into others through projective identification. Those surrounding depressed people, including therapists, introject these depressive feelings or psychic parts, and, in turn, become depressed. Nevertheless, these depressive bits are alien to the therapist and can be recognized as such. This recognition brings relief for the therapist and staff from the, hopefully, transitory depressions that are created by patients. Sometimes the personal life experiences of therapists and staff make them especially vulnerable to the depressive symptoms created by particular patients. These can be worked upon by self-analysis in the ongoing therapeutic process with the patient or client.

Patients, in turn, are depressed by others. Certain patients are chosen in families or in groups to be the scapegoat and carry the depressive affects of the others. This may continue when they choose partners or involve themselves in situations where they carry, as part of their unconscious roles, the depressive feelings that are put into them by other people. Sometimes the projective identificatory parts, which are, of course, unconscious, evoke fatigue and hypochondriasis in others who are the recipients. The therapist may suffer in this way.

Patients will react to others in ways that have to be interpreted. They will deny what is being done to them psychologically, or become derisory when they are threatened by loss of their self-control. When they are depressed they will affect those of us who care for them. Depression threatens *our* narcissism and self-esteem. We react by denial, disavowal, and contempt. We develop a sense of mastery and control and a sense of triumph, since they, not we, are involved. Our own manic defenses (Melanie Klein) have to be scrutinized and worked with, just as we have to interpret theirs.

5

Group
Psychodynamics:
the Patient
and the Therapist

We move almost constantly from one group to another. These groups may be work units, hospital committees, case conferences, sports teams, and so on. Each one of us, therefore, is affected by the psychodynamics of small and large groups. Patients and clients bring to their individual therapy the problems of the groups of which they are a part. Therapists, also, live and work in groups and they, too, are influenced by similar group psychological processes. How all these influences, commonly viewed as extraneous, affect patients and therapists and their work together has been a neglected area of investigation.

In a panel, "Psychoanalytic Knowledge of Group Processes," reported by Calder (1979), the chairman, Burness E. Moore, suggested that a possible reason for the neglect of the study of group processes is that analysts are better equipped, by predilection and training, to deal with individual therapy. According to Moore, analysts are disturbed by questions that invariably result in modifications in theory when fundamental psychoanalytic concepts derived from a dyadic relationship are adapted to groups. Moore suggests that possibly "a neglect of the study of groups represents a defence against the affects, especially anxiety, evoked by our own group processes—related to regression, conflict, and a release of aggression—which threaten disruption of the group and consequent separation from ambivalently regarded others."

FREUD'S CONCEPTS

Freud (1921) in "Group Psychology and the Analysis of the Ego" had great influence upon the early psychoanalytic study of group psychodynamics. Unfortunately, his work was translated as "group psychology" rather than the more appropriate "mass psychology."

Freud believed that individuals in "groups" establish a sense of togetherness or intimacy with one another by projecting their ego ideals onto the leader and, individually, becoming identified with the leader as well as with each other by such a process. Because of the projection of the ego ideals onto the then-idealized leader, constraints of a moral nature and the higher functions of self-criticism and responsibility (now regarded as being regulated by the superego) are lessened or eliminated. Members of the "group" are prevented from losing their sense of identity by the sense of unity and belonging that results from such projective mechanisms. There is, however, a reduction of ego functioning, and primitive unconscious needs take over. The "group" then functions under the influence of instinctual drives. Affects occur, such as excitement or rage, that may be stimulated, directed, and controlled by the leader.

Freud based some of these concepts on LeBon's idea of the primal horde. He cited the organization of the church and the army as examples of such mechanisms, but it should be remembered that Freud had never been a member of either of these. His own experiences of groups came from the psychoanalytic movement and presumably from hearing about other organizations from his patients.

BION'S CONCEPTS

In the late 'forties, Bion studied groups (see Bion 1961) in an experiential fashion. He gathered together and observed small groups whose primary aim was to try to understand what the unconscious forces were that diverted them from their main task, which Bion designated the "work task" of the group. These studies, it should be noted, were with what are defined as "small groups," groups, that is, where individuals sit down and meet each other face to face. Such groups are composed of six to sixteen members. Below that number Bion felt that individual personalities continued to stand out; with more than that one experienced different types of group psychodynamics.

Bion observed that such a small group, sitting down to a "work task," would, quite unintentionally and without conscious awareness, shift the group pattern in a collusive way among the members onto a different task. He observed these patterns were *as if* the group were working on a *different assumed task*. Bion referred to these types of groups as "basic assumption groups." They operate in an "as if" situation. The group is behaving "as if" the situation to be dealt with were another one.

By studying their patterns of behavior, Bion observed that there were three distinct types of basic assumption groups. These he named the Basic Assumption Dependent Group, the Basic Assumption Fight-Flight Group, and the Basic Assumption Pairing Group.

The Dependent Group

The most common type of Basis Assumption Group is what Bion called the Dependent Group (for an overview, see Rioch 1970).

In this type of group a powerful individual takes on the role of leader. Although he or she may not be consciously delineated as such, the leader is felt by the group to be omniscient and omnipotent. The others hang on his or her word, expecting to be provided for. The rest of the membership lose the skills they have, their critical faculties, their capacity for action, and regress to helplessness and dependency. There is a great deal of conformity and contentment in the group—and a resentment of interpretations that might disturb this familiar comfort—and an air of timelessness, which is a characteristic of dependency. The group feels no urgency to set goals and objectives. Its aim is, in a collusive way, to provide security for its members, rather than to get anything done. Casualties may arise in such groups, whereupon the group will rally around to look after the person who has problems, who is psychologically wounded, and so on (the mental health group may worry about the failing trainee, for example).

Sometimes the "leader," whose function is to maintain security, may not, in fact, be a person but may be a "bible," a history, a routine, a "way of doing things."

The Fight-Flight Group

Fight-Flight is the name Bion gives to a second pattern of group behavior. Here the aim of the group is to discharge the tension within the group. There is the fantasy, sometimes conscious, sometimes an unconscious phantasy, that something unpredictable is going to happen and that there is need for action, not for thought. The group is not introspective and is unlikely to search for knowledge. It has no concern for the possible consequences of its action. It may encourage heroics.

A Fight-Flight group takes some time to consolidate, since members of such a group need to know each other.

The Pairing Group

Bion named his third type of Basic Assumption group the Pairing Group. The aim of this group is to create. It wishes to reproduce itself. Such a group becomes preoccupied with preservation, without questioning the need for preservation. Such groups have an air of hopeful expectation. There is the idea that "hope will arise out of the ashes." There may be an actual "coupling" among members of the group, as if such a thing as a marriage will solve the problems of existence. Bion brilliantly points out that the leader of this group is not within the group, but is a person or idea *outside* the group who will come and save it. The leader, be it a person or idea, never comes because to have to deal with a real person or real concept might lead to disillusionment. Such a group, with its air of hope, sometimes evolves so its members might escape confronting work that is depressing.

The Work Group

The Work Group is the term Bion gives to groups that perform effectively the primary task for which they have met. The group has a grasp of reality. The members consciously cooperate, and exercise their intelligence and forbearance. Skills are used, and the roles of the members of the group are related to its avowed aims, which are clearly defined. Rational procedures of examining, predicting, and testing hypotheses, for example, are used, and the members of the group learn by experience. In the Work Group the "leader" is the member of the group whose skills are most relevant to the task at any given moment. The true leadership changes as the group goes about its work. The group may incorporate some basic activity—"pairing," for example, if a certain amount of esprit de corps is helpful to the work.

In management theory, in industry and business, terms other than "work group," such as "management-by-objectives," may be used.

Bion believes that while there are basic assumption factors operating in all groups, the level of these varies between groups to different degrees. The role of the individual in participating in basic assumption activities also varies and is determined through what Bion calls "valence."

Turquet (1974) defines the concept of the primary task. The Work Group, he says, is activated by a desire to know, to acquire insights and explanations, and to test hypotheses. Turquet believes that an important distinguishing feature of a Work Group is the freedom to associate that is enjoyed by its members. They are also free to resign, and this freedom is not a threat to themselves or to the group. If a group has a structure—chairman, secretary, and the like—the structure is related to the needs of the primary task. The chairman's role, for example, is to facilitate the rapid shift of leadership from one person in the group to another.

TURQUET'S ONENESS GROUP

Turquet added a fourth category, the Basic Assumption Oneness Group, where members seek to join in a powerful union with an omnipotent force, unobtainably high, to surrender the self for passive participation and thereby feel existence, well being, and wholeness.

Turquet's concept of the Basic Assumption Oneness

Group has not really caught on. How members surrender their "basic selves," I feel, is common to all those in small and large groups. The feeling of existence, well being, and wholeness seems to be prevalent in other types of small groups, described by Bion and others.

OTHER GROUP CONCEPTS

Kernberg (1989) describes how Anzieu and Chasseguet-Smirgel build upon Bion's and Turquet's work. Anzieu describes some of the ad hoc ideologies that emerge under regressive conditions in both large and small groups. Where there is a lack of structure, the group as a whole acquires characteristics of fusion of their "individual instinctive needs with a fantastic conception of the group as a primitive ego ideal, equated to an all-gratifying primary object, the mother of the earliest stages of development" (Kernberg 1989, p. 200). Anzieu points out the shared illusion that the group is constituted by individuals who are all equal (thus denying sexual differences and castration anxiety), that the group is self-engendered and might solve all narcissistic lesions. The group becomes an idealized "breast-mother." Chasseguet-Smirgel expands upon Anzieu by suggesting that the group selects leadership that "represents not the paternal aspects of the prohibitive superego, but a pseudo paternal 'promoter of illusions' which provides the group with an ideology that confirms the narcissistic aspirations of fusion of the individual within the group as a primitive ego ideal, the all-powerful, all-gratifying pre-oedipal mother" (Kernberg 1989, p. 200).

Kernberg goes on to suggest that the psychoanalytic study of group processes points to mechanisms of immediate regression of individuals in mobs and unstructured large and small groups. He feels that this explains why groups are characterized by superego regression, narcissistic orientation, paranoid developments, and a general pressure toward conformity. He also believes that there exists group formation prompted by the sheer pleasure of the regressive experience of being part of the group process.

Arlow (in Calder 1979) remarks upon the continuity and contiguity of elements under discussion in groups, which could be approached in a manner comparable to the organization of data observed in the free associations of an individual in psychoanalytic therapy. When an individual is in a group, that is to say, he or she picks up the thread from a previous individual who has spoken, so that a common unconscious continuity occurs. Ezriel (1957) suggests that the apparently disconnected thoughts, affects, and actions of individuals in a group belong together dynamically at any time: they are meaningfully related and arise from a common unconscious source. A remark made by a member clicks because in some way it is relevant to, and can fit into, the ongoing dominant unconscious phantasies of the rest. It is taken up by the others and becomes the unconsciously determined topic of the group. It is the common denominator of the dominant unconscious phantasies of all the members. Each individual group member will deal with the common group tension in his or her own particular way, but the group becomes structured so that the object relations of each individual member conforms to the common group tension.

Calder (1979) remarks on the basic threat to personal identity in group processes. Group processes, he asserts, have a predisposition to activate primitive object relations, primitive defensive operations, and crude aggression. These are part and parcel of the group experience.

Zaleznik, in the panel cited above, however, counters that formal organizations aid, indeed coerce, individuals to suppress intrapsychic conflict, limit interpersonal conflict, and control the expression of affect in order to concentrate energies and attention upon the purposive activities of the organization. He considers regressions in organizations to be "noise in the system," to be contained by the use of power if necessary. He seems to feel that other theories, such as Game Theory, functional analysis, and bureaucratic power-relations may be of more use to organizations than understanding of group processes. My own experience as a consultant is to the contrary. Many organizations, committees, boards, and so forth function not on a work task basis, but are often infused with basic assumption activity. One of the main consulting tasks, therefore, is to help mobilize individuals, particularly those in designated authority, to become reskilled to act in a work-oriented fashion.

EFFECTS UPON A THERAPIST

One form of the de-skilling that must be reversed is often that caused by depression in the individuals who are ineffectively struggling with the group task or who are scapegoated and depressed by other group members. Occasionally, of course, individuals may be especially affected because the group task, or the common unconscious phantasy (Ezriel) is related to experiences, fantasies, or phantasies in their personal, private world.

> Max, a senior psychiatric resident, came for supervision in what he admitted was a very depressed state. He had been seriously affected by an unproductive and highly emotional meeting about child abuse held in the Child Unit.
> Child abuse is a serious matter and is not to be taken lightly. Dealing with it requires work-oriented thinking about causes, effects, how the cases can be treated, their occurrence minimized, and so on, not regressive emotional responses. Max conceded, however, that after the case conference others

were not as overwhelmed as he was himself. The supervisor delicately questioned why this should be so; why he personally suffered so much more than the level of affect in his peers.

Max revealed to his supervisor, with some difficulty, that he had endured a certain amount of emotional abuse by his parents in his early years. He was in personal therapy and this was being worked on. It is most likely, therefore, that Max was affected, probably quite appropriately, as were others in the case conference, but the residual effects were more intense within Max for the next few days because of his own personal early life experiences. The discussion of physical child abuse had resonated within him his own preconscious fantasies about incidents from his own childhood, which he tried to keep out of his mind.

Health care professionals, however, often have to meet within their organization to settle matters of horrendous nature and general concern. Often these pressures lead to regression and collusion among group members to handle the depressive feelings latent when serious health problems are discussed, and the members have to deal, on a work-directed basis, with problems that may appear insoluble. We must remember, too, that many mental health unit diagnoses, treatment plans, and nursing and social work programs are formulated in committees, which are small groups and subject to small group psychodynamics (Heath 1971). Let us consider, therefore, the value of Bion's models of basic assumption groups, where the group engages in activity different from the work task, by looking at specific cases. These examples also indicate how individuals who treat patients or clients may be affected by others with whom they work.

Kenneth was a competent junior staff psychiatrist in a teaching hospital, who discussed a number of cases in supervision. But one case in particular depressed him profoundly. Kenneth had to treat a woman who had come into therapy to help her come to terms with as yet uncontrollable and unresolved grief over the loss of her child in a tragic accident. The tragedy was reported in the local newspapers, and well-meaning relatives and friends talked to her about it repeatedly, bombarded her with questions, and added their grief and anger to her own. Her therapy showed her what she had difficulty accepting at first, that she not only grieved but harbored enormous rage toward the driver of the car that had killed her child. She became more deeply depressed when the driver received what she thought was a minor sentence for his alleged crime.

Kenneth described the case, and his own despair and difficulty in treating the woman, to his supervisor. He also recounted his presenting of the patient in a case conference in the psychiatric outpatient department unit. He had hoped for help. Instead, his telling of the story of the therapy and his attempts to deal with the woman's rage and intense grief aroused similar reactions in his listeners. They formed what Bion would call a Fight Group. Their talk moved far from the boundaries of a case discussion: the driver of the car should be punished or hurt. They recalled other instances when sentences had been too light. There should be more stringent testing of automobiles. Then the case conference shifted into a depressed Dependent Group, where even the senior consultant was depressed by the discussion of the case and, in turn, immobilized.

The patient suffered a severe depression in reaction to a tragedy. The patient's depression depressed the therapist. The therapist sought help by discussing his case at the outpatient case conference, but his narrative and depression inadvertently created an angry, then a depressed case-conference small group. The case discussion was not in any way related to a solution to Kenneth's problems in treating the woman, and came up with no productive ideas. There was *no* Work Group (Bion 1961).

The task of the supervisor, who agreed that it was difficult to be unaffected by the narrative of the woman's tragedy, was to strengthen the psychological boundaries between

Kenneth and his patient. He had to emphasize that the tragedy was that of Kenneth's patient and not of Kenneth himself. The therapist could empathize with the patient, with the terrible nature of what had happened and the circumstances surrounding it, but it was important for him to maintain a psychological distance from her and not be overwhelmed by sympathy, which is a very different thing. Sympathy means overidentification with a patient. Kenneth had put himself into the patient and was thereby experiencing the tragedy on an "as if" basis, "as if" it were his own. By changing from a sympathetic to an empathetic orientation, Kenneth was able to pull back from his case psychologically, to understand his patient and not be overwhelmed by the depression in her. She was no longer able to project her massive depression into him in a projective identificatory way and thereby put him into psychological overload.

Odette was a 26-year-old woman admitted to an inpatient unit with what was diagnosed as a schizo-affective disorder. Confused and paranoid, an important part of her symptomatology was an acute depression. Because of her history of suicidal attempts, and as a result of the case discussion, it was decided to place her under close observation with round-the-clock nursing supervision.

Odette was supposedly under constant observation and in intense individual therapy with a psychiatric resident who was in close touch with the nursing, occupational, and social work staff, as well as with his own staff psychiatrist. Ward notes included comments about her that suggested that this constant observation was being maintained and that she was in her room. All the staff, and the resident, seemed oblivious to the fact that Odette was, in fact, spending most of her time wandering around other wards of the hospital. Even more surprising, the resident, although he was vaguely aware of this, presumably in his preconscious, acted as if nothing untoward was happening. This patient, for whom he was responsible, was out of sight of the staff on her ward for most of the day, except during her sessions with him. The situation became so serious to others in the hospital that it was necessary for other members of the psychiatric staff to set up special case conferences to discuss the problem. It became apparent that Odette was a very depressed, possibly suicidal, woman who had created the impression that nothing, absolutely nothing, could be done to help her. She seemed to sense, however, that she was in need of some kind of protection so that in her wanderings she never left the psychiatric section of the hospital, and touched base with various wards and their nursing teams. She was so depressing that everyone with whom she came in contact backed away. Most especially she depressed the nursing and ancillary teams and the resident in psychiatry on the ward where she was supposed to be under constant observation.

Those responsible for Odette's care exhibited the characteristics of Bion's Flight Group. The patient and her psychosis led the group to take flight, unconsciously, from the depression they evoked. The group ignored and neglected to care for her. Special case conferences were set up with the specific aim of delineating the group's primary tasks in relation to the care of Odette, apportioning responsibilities, and creating of them a Work Group. Odette was then placed under *truly* constant observation.

While this is an extreme example, it is unlikely that it is an isolated case. Case conferences themselves, when they are work oriented, may decrease the psychological pressures upon those in the mental health field. Shifting the members of a ward team into maximum ego functioning can be valuable and probably therapeutic. Such case conferences may also help to maintain the psychological boundaries between individual health practitioners and their patients and thereby deter them from, consciously or unconsciously, building barriers (which are not the same as boundaries) between themselves and the very difficult patients with whom they may have to deal.

The number of groups in the medical and social science fields, as, indeed, in most areas of human activity dependent upon an autocratic leader or upon a system that is long past its usefulness, is legion. One example will suffice.

Marilyn, a social worker with an impressive reputation, a highly intelligent but somewhat controlling person, was appointed director of a Children's Care Unit. The government-sponsored and funded unit was designed to fill a gap in the community resources of a small city. Marilyn skillfully amalgamated two smaller clinics, with their social workers and psychologists, into the new unit and hired four enthusiastic junior psychiatric social workers. A psychiatric resident rotated from a nearby university teaching hospital as part of his community health training. It soon became apparent that although his supervisor was elsewhere, he was expected to report to Marilyn: a division of authority and responsibility that was unclear to his supervisor at the university and himself.

The new clinic suffered growing pains. It was bombarded with referrals. Inexperienced secretarial support staff found dealing with telephone calls from various other agencies or local physicians about disturbed youngsters too personally distressing. Perhaps Marilyn was the wrong choice for a hastily assembled unit. She dealt with its problems by exercising tight control over all her staff. The staff themselves were facing major readjustments. The older ones had to adjust to Marilyn's methods; the new ones had, seemingly, to try to forget what they had learned at university. All became deskilled and depressed. When they experienced depressive feelings about the situation, Marilyn resolved them in one-on-one meetings where she gave advice.

The group rapidly shifted into a highly dependent relationship with Marilyn. Soon each member was approaching her repeatedly for instructions on all matters. Even the psychi-

atric resident asked her for supervision. The secretaries re-
quested and got a small manual on how she wanted referrals to
be handled. There was little input from the rest of the staff,
though staff meetings went on endlessly. Marilyn complained
that her staff were like children who could not survive without
her.

Eventually things settled down. Routines evolved; there
was an air of calm. The backlog of referrals developed into an
extensive waiting list, and was rationalized as the community's problem. Complaints from members of the community
were dismissed with statements such as, "They don't understand how much we have to do," and not addressed by staff
members in the expectation that Marilyn would deal with all
of them. The resident reported that he had settled in and
enjoyed the unhurried atmosphere there, in contrast to that of
the university hospital. Marilyn provided perks for the staff—
funds for educational conferences and the like.

Marilyn was difficult to deal with at times, especially for
the junior social workers, who often complained that they
were doing directive counseling and not the psychodynamic
psychotherapy that they wished to do and for which they had
been trained. One adapted. The others left, feeling frustrated
and depressed. The rest of the group expressed relief at the
departure of the alleged "troublemakers."

From time to time other individual members became
angry and depressed by Marilyn's strict regime and by the
sense that they were underusing their skills. They either had to
adjust or leave.

Ironically, it was only after Marilyn's promotion and
transfer to a larger clinic that the problems of the Children's
Care Unit became apparent to the new director, many of
whose staff longed for "the good old days."

The wealthy parents of a handicapped adolescent felt
there was a gap in available residential facilities for the handicapped young. They assembled several highly intelligent and

highly educated people to set up a foundation to create such a residence, to be financed with private and, hopefully, public resources. A prominent architect volunteered to join the group and draw up plans for the building. The building he designed was very beautiful, architecturally reminiscent of a private mansion, and had many desirable rehabilitation facilities, but it was one whose construction costs promised to be extraordinarily high. The plans were trimmed down, and the high expectations of the group remained undiminished, despite the fact that the modified buildling would still be an expensive one. A site was bought on the edge of a large city in a wooded ravine.

Within the meetings, murmured concerns about the construction costs and large proposed operating budget were diverted to enthusiastic discussion of the benefits to be derived from the building, which would be a model for future units throughout the state, and the beauty of the location.

One young woman, tragically paralyzed from the waist down, spoke of how "graduates" of the Foundation would be able to travel throughout the area showing what the handicapped could do, in unique (but unspecified) ways. Applause greeted her remarks. Rooms in the facility were to be double ones and there was lively, somewhat premature, discussion of how the occupants would not necessarily be segregated on the basis of their sex. One management consultant who suggested the project might be an unusually expensive marriage bureau was not invited back.

Here we see an example of what Bion called a Pairing Group. The atmosphere was one of great hope and expectation. Doubts about costs of construction and operation were dismissed with idealogical statements about the proposal being "a showpiece." The members of the group that met to initiate the project talked about the handicapped "graduating" from the facility, not recognizing the severe lifelong physical problems that would probably ensure that they would be resident there for life.

The true leader of this group was an ideology—a new way of doing things that would produce magical results. It was an ideology that permitted massive denial of the depressive feelings about the tragic reality of the situation of the handicapped young people. Had these feelings been acknowledged and worked through, the talented and powerful people co-opted might have formed a Work Group that produced something of real use. Certainly there was need for a facility for handicapped young adults. As it was, private funding proved inadequate, the government thought the project too extravagant, interest and enthusiasm for it gradually faded, and the executive director, realizing that it had become unrealistic, with much sadness on the part of all concerned, disbanded the group.

GROUP EFFECTS UPON A THERAPIST AND HIS PATIENTS

Bion emphasized that his models were derived from studies of small groups where individuals met in face-to-face situations. Implicit in the Pairing Group is an idea, or a messiah, that is not, actually, of the group itself, but Bion did not elaborate on this—nor, to my knowledge, has anyone else. My own view is that individuals constantly carry in their minds "the groups" to which they belong, and it is the "group in the mind" with which we are concerned. Thus I would extend the definition of groups beyond face-to-face situations.

Bill was a middle-aged psychoanalyst in his second analysis. He described meetings he was attending with his peers, senior psychiatrists from various theoretical and training backgrounds, to hear one of their number report on negotiations being conducted with an insurance company that proposed making changes in psychiatric health insurance benefits, changes that were likely to put major restrictions on the psychiatrists' work. While the exact details are not important, the essence of the insurance company's plan was to put a limit on the number of psychotherapy sessions that might be given by the providers to their patients. The implications of the proposed changes were worrying and depressing to the dozen or so psychiatrists at the meetings. What would happen to the patients when the insurance benefits stopped? As many of the patients were not wealthy, paying for further treatment themselves would constitute considerable financial hardship. Would they have expectations of the therapists, and would the physicians have the obligation to continue treating them without charge? What effect would this have on treatment, treatment process, and, most likely, on treatment progress? More practically, how would the therapists afford it? While they worked out some negotiating strategies and tactics, essentially a feeling of depressive helplessness prevailed in the group.

Bill wondered how long he and his colleagues would be able to practice psychotherapy. He worried that he might have difficulty getting patients. He worried about the likely reduction in his income and its effect upon the life of his family. He had two children in university; their tuition, room, and board were major expenditures from his earnings. He himself had had an impoverished boyhood and this added to the rage and impotence he felt, as all his colleagues felt in their dealings with the insurance company, and contributed to a reactive depression.

Bill recognized this all too clearly. He noticed that after one of his meetings with his group of colleagues his feelings about his patients changed. He said that he began to care less about his work and about those he treated, blaming them for being of the society of which the insurance company was a part. His lack of sleep was disrupting his work. He admitted that too often he was not listening to patient material and was missing things. His patients, some of whom perceived this, remarked that he seemed to have "changed." They wondered if he had a serious, even terminal, illness. (We can speculate that this was an expression of their unconscious angry reactions to him: that they were wishing that he were dead because his various omissions caused them to feel that he was, psychologically, abandoning them). It is important to recognize that we are dealing with a depressed therapist, who at other times was a conscientious, good physician who functioned normally. In this particular phase of his professional life Bill was profoundly depressed by matters beyond his control, and his depression was particularly acute after meeting with his group of peers.

After Bill's meetings with his colleagues, some of Bill's patients reported that for some inexplicable reason they did not seem to be functioning very well in their lives. This led Bill in his personal analysis to muse about what was going on. It was possible to make links to early issues in his childhood that were being reactivated by the current situation. These were related to the withdrawal of care of him by his mother when his father was in the military and away. One could, therefore, make interpretations about material in his early life that was related to his current depressive affect. Nonetheless, it was possible also to point out that he was carrying away introjections of depression from his group meetings, which so profoundly affected him that he, in turn, was affecting his work with his patients. Some of these patients were becoming depressed and disjointed in their own therapy sessions with him. Patients would remark to Bill that he was bothering them, that he seemed to be depressed or that he was depressing them, that he focused on unpleasant aspects of their lives and did not see anything positive, and so on. Bill's analyst suggested that, by projective identification, he was "unloading" in an anal way some of the depression into his patients in an effort to expel the "mental feces," his depressive symptomatology, which he carried from the meetings with his colleagues. His analyst was able to make "here-and-now" interpretations about what was going on in the transference: that, similarly, Bill was making unconscious attempts to depress his analyst by projecting his depression into him and unconsciously bring his analyst into the group he was working with in the outside setting.

These interpretations had a major effect upon Bill. He

began to see how he was internalizing and introjecting paranoid anxiety and depressive anxieties from his past (thereby
from his internal objects) and his present (the external objects,
the members of his psychological group of colleagues, and the
external objects of those who were causing them difficulties).

Small group dynamics also operate when individuals are
in contact with one another by satellite, telephone links, daily
communications, and so on. More important, as I have said, I
believe that individuals carry "the groups" to which they
belong in their minds almost all the time. They carry the
psychological work and the relationship to the members
throughout the day and in their dreams, and other unconscious workings, at night. Thus I would extend the definition
of groups beyond face-to-face situations to reflect this reality.
When we look at large groups, where individuals cannot meet
constantly in a face-to-face situation, we shall see the extension is clear.

MEDIUM-SIZED GROUPS

The psychodynamics of groups begin to change when the
people in them number more than twenty. In these larger
groups individuals no longer see each other face to face or
conceptualize the group as a whole. Gradually, with a bare
beginning of blurring of individual personalities, the change
from small group dynamics into the psychodynamics of
groups containing forty members or more takes place. There
may be fractions or splits of the group to form small groups.

THE PSYCHODYNAMICS
OF LARGE GROUPS

Knowledge of the psychodynamics of large groups comes
from a number of sources including studies of large groups in

clinical and managerial situations. Those pertinent to a psychoanalytic approach are summarized by Kreeger (1975). A valuable source is from the study of large groups in conferences put on by the Tavistock Institute of Human Relations in London, England, and held at the University of Leicester, and by the A. K. Rice Institute of the Washington School of Psychiatry, Washington, DC. These conferences consist of a number of events, in one of which approximately sixty members of the conference sit and study what goes on in the group.

Kernberg (1989), from experiences in conferences and in consulting work, suggests that in such groups there is projection of superego functions, which results in a simplistic, conventional black-or-white morality. He proposes that the temporary loss of a sense of identity by the individuals in large groups (which I shall come to later) carries with it a temporary loss of the higher level of autonomous abstract and superego functions as well. At the same time, he asserts, there is a regression to the functioning of the latency child superego and this latency superego is projected to the group at large. This is not my observation, nor that of others in such conferences.

ALIENATION IN LARGE GROUPS

Individuals feel isolated and alienated within meetings of large groups. Turquet explains this phenomenon by means of the Kleinian concept of projective identification. In phantasy, part of an individual's psyche is put into another person who may, consciously or unconsciously, receive it, and so introject the individual's psychic bit. The first person may then take back the part. This taking back is "introjection." As we discussed earlier, some suggest that synthetic function parts of the ego can be projected as well (see the chapter on countertransference). Turquet argues that projective identification is the basis of reality testing in any situation: one puts bits of oneself into another person then takes them back to see if they match up to one's expectations. If there is a fit, then the taking back gives one an idea of what the other person is like. Turquet suggests that this is a constant, ongoing process. When we identify with an object, we feel we would like to be that object (this can even include an inanimate object and is the process that gives "understanding" of that thing).

Now picture an individual entering a large group of forty or more people. Whereas when one joins a small group one can take in at a glance each of those who are there, when the group is a large one, one cannot. Turquet theorizes that in large groups the individual's projective identificatory parts go out but they do not come back to him or her as they do in simple one-to-one relationships or in small groups where the members can identify one another. Rather, they get lost in the confusion. Thus begins the process of alienation. Each individual has lost parts of him- or herself into the other members. Each one, therefore, has a tendency to feel denuded of parts. Each feels emptied, psychologically.

HOMOGENIZATION

According to Turquet, since all members of the large group share the feeling that they have become denuded of psychic parts of themselves, they all feel very much the same and that they have become equal. Because everyone is felt to be alike, there is a lessening of struggles for power. Turquet says this homogenization is a defense against power struggles in large groups.

Unfortunately, in large groups, there is a great deal of frustration, with resulting tensions and confusion. The psychic parts that are projected are the unwanted ones, such as hostile feelings or confusion. The individual, then, finds him-

or herself in a roomful of people all of whom appear confused, strange, threatening, and so forth. He or she experiences a further sense of isolation, some rupture of internal boundaries. Thus there is the threat that all of the bizarreness, confusion, background noise, and so on may come rushing into him or her. This leads the individual to retreat yet further and into him- or herself. Some become depressed as a reaction to the group, or by introjection of others' depression about their inability to exercise control.

Members of large groups attempt to compensate for the sense of depletion and alienation. Some will retreat into themselves as a way of keeping self-control and a sense of self. Others will sit in large group meetings with people they know and attempt to form pairs, to form simple relationships to provide some internal psychological stability for themselves. (Almost everyone, incidently, after taking his or her seat in a theater will look around to see if there is anyone he or she recognizes.) For further protection, small group clusters form, particularly where there is a common background: groups of women, of professionals, of Californians, say.

In Tavistock Group Relations Conferences, some members have been observed to exhibit bizarre behavior that suggested that they were trying to protect themselves from threats to their sense of self and the alienation processes. Some become so threatened that they have to leave the meetings. Many of us in large groups find ourselves speaking in an assertive manner. We do this to maintain our internal sense of identity. The views we so forcefully espouse may be quite different from those we hold before and after the meetings.

THE CLINIC AS A GROUP

I would extend the definition of the large group to include organizations that may consist of forty to more than sixty

people, even though these people may work with walls between them, so that subunits are formed. In organizations of
this size, in industry, in the social services, in psychiatric or
clinical institutions assertive behavior is not uncommon. This
behavior is, basically, an attempt by individuals to maintain
their identity, which is threatened by group processes.

It is interesting that while meetings (or organizations)
may be quite chaotic, individuals within their own subunits
where they have maintained their own identity or sense of self
can function well. Main (1975) points out that after chaotic
large group meetings in his clinical setting at The Cassel
Hospital in England, individuals would re-form in small
groups to discuss them. Main feels that there was some kind of
return to sanity within these small groups. He maintains that
this habit of meeting afterwards in small groups was necessary
even for senior staff or consultants to assess the large group
meetings and work out just what had gone on.

WAVES OF PROJECTIVE IDENTIFICATION

Turquet and I have observed that sometimes there seem to be
waves of affects connected with ideas that "move" across the
meeting. An individual picks up and speaks what another has
said, and elaborates upon it, adding a certain amount of
emotional tone. This is done again and again and again so that
one can see what appears to be a wave effect of changes in
content of cumulative emotional experience, which moves
from one person to another across a large group meeting
(sometimes even back and forth). As chairman of a public
forum on psychoanalysis, I observed with fascination that a
point made in the audience was picked up by another person
and elaborated upon, and this was done by yet a third person
until it was repeated several times and finally addressed to a
member of the panel on the platform. Similar experiences are

very common in the presentations and discussions of scientific papers in large group meetings. Criticism or laughter may occur in common waves across the audience, repeated and added to, sometimes with little verbal content, until the wave has landed forcefully upon the presenter.

There is, then, a great deal of background bombardment in large groups. The individual in them has to deal with waves of feeling, confusion, and rapidly changing or altering ideas, moving back and forth. Similarly, in the extension of the defined large group, in the association, the clinic, the department, members experience the same sweep through the unit of ideas, rumors, and emotions being added to and modified.

"NOBEL PRIZE THINKING"

Main (1975) observes that in his clinical setting, in community meetings of patients and staff in a mental health unit, participants would attempt to assert their individuality, but become very abstract in their thinking. He terms this type of behavior "Nobel Prize Thinking" and suggests that members of large groups become less specific in their thinking and expression to defend their identity and render it less vulnerable to criticism or attack. "Nobel Prize Thinking," he suggests, is based upon the projection of the ego ideal of individual members. Main describes how, particularly when the task of the group meeting was not clearly defined, members would produce and develop elaborate abstract theories. In scientific and political meetings, too, conceptualization often soars to lofty planes with the tacit approval of the total membership. Members collude and even contribute to the generalizations without any evaluation of each others' contribution to the total work. It is possible that such a form of intellectualization is a cover for depression in group members.

Main observed further that another form of abstraction

occurred in some of his large group meetings. After a while members would begin to talk about "The Group," as if it were an entity in itself. Sometimes "The Group" would feel like a cloud hanging over the meeting, directing and mobilizing it. Questions and discussions would address it rather than remarks made by particular members about any subtask or part of the organization itself.

This phenomenon is a way of handling fantasies (conscious) and, presumably, phantasies (unconscious) about the *power* of a large group. Main suggests that while it, too, is a projection of the ego ideal of individual members, it is also an attempt to contain the confusion of a large group meeting. Unfortunately, it leads to further depersonalization as the individual then has to deal with a powerful abstraction hanging over him as he attempts to work upon the tasks.

At times in the history of psychoanalysis we have observed references to "psychoanalysis," and the need to preserve and promote it, when psychoanalysts in the particular community are feeling under pressure and are depressed.

EXECUTIVES IN LARGE GROUPS

Whatever the task and milieu of the large group meeting the role of the executive of it is difficult. Executives or consultants are subject to the same forces as the general membership. They are bombarded with and are receptacles for the same projections that others in the group put into them, and they, in turn, introject, project, and take back in. Some try to maintain their identity by forming small groups, as if they, as executives, are different from the membership. They, too, may get caught up in "Nobel Prize Thinking" and become ponderous. They may address remarks to "The Clinic" or "The Institute" or "The

Company" or whatever, as Main has described. These generalities may also be the administrator's defense against personal depression over the work, or coping with the group.

MYTHS

Myths are said to develop in large group meetings because there are no traditions. Traditions may be referred to, but in large group meetings there is little sense of carryover from one meeting to another. Members become tied up with anxiety and confusion and turn to their traditional roles in groupings prior to their joining these present ones. Group myths emerge that are said to be about the handling of violence.

When the members are confused they try to project their confusion out of themselves. They then experience the total meeting as confused, and this leads to an internal reaction of frustration and aggression. This reaction may lead them to angrily reject others or to use other members to handle the group vicariously or to verbalize, on their behalf, their frustrations and reactions to the group.

A common myth is that of the power of the large group. Some large groups are very frightening. From the point of view of the individuals in them, the tension and frustration in them seem to have no boundaries, checks, or controls. Particular individuals, therefore, may take over the leadership of them, and lead them in ways unrelated to the group's task. They may hold promise of "a new way of doing things," which will resolve many of the organizational problems of the institution.

Mumby (1975) feels that large group meetings are significant in industry. They help pull an industrial organization together and provide a sense of cohesion, which is in itself good. Struggling through wars, real or psychological, may tie individuals together in a common bond.

Institutions, in contrast to large group meetings, have traditions. Instead, myths develop around individuals to handle depression about the way the organization is functioning. An example might be that the previous director could have resolved a particular issue that is depressing a number of the present staff, if only he or she were still within the organization.

In large groups individuals are scapegoated. Then there is the fantasy that all will be well if only the group or organization rids itself of that particular individual. In clinical situations this may mean passing on a particularly difficult or depressed patient to another hospital, or transferring a patient or client to another therapist who has been mythologized into one who is "the person able to treat these kinds of people." In the same way some staff are scapegoated and evicted from an organization.

LEADERSHIP

Leadership does sometimes emerge in large groups, and rational procedures can be brought to bear in them. Sometimes this leadership is sanctioned into a form of knighthood with the collusion of many of the members of the group. The kind of leader so ennobled by the group is usually one who will accept the common denominator, who will not "rock the boat." This compliance may be necessary to the development of an organization at a particular time, of course, but sometimes it is not.

Some individuals may be lionized and cast in the role of the one who is near perfect. They are so perceived for only a limited time, however. In some organizations such individuals attempt to take on the role. They overwork to maintain themselves in it, and bask in the limelight of being scape-graced. Such a leadership incites envy (a particularly destructive quality in itself), and, should the leader assert his individuality, and behave in ways not sanctioned by the group, he or she may well find the process is reversed, that he or she is denigrated and scapegoated. Our clinical work in therapy with mental health professionals often deals with the depressed casualties created in or evicted from care-giving institutions (which may be viewed as large groups subject to large group psychodynamics).

INSTITUTIONALIZATION

This is described by theorists as one of the most efficient defenses against violent fantasies and phantasies in the large group. It evolves sometimes in the election of such individuals as chairpersons, secretaries, and the like. Such an impersonality may lead to a further isolation of the individual. When the leaders are so institutionalized it is the servants who are first to the firing line (Turquet 1975). The individual elevated to leadership may be so concerned about running the group and maintaining its systems that he or she may not be open to understanding and insights. Robert's Rules of Order can make for efficiency but they can also be used in such a way that real discussion or expression of feelings about issues never takes place.

INTERPRETATIONS

Main argues that one should never interpret to "The Group," because to do so only adds further to its creation. Others would disagree with his contention that one has no contract to make psychoanalytic interpretations to large groups. Certainly it is not easy to make a simple interpretation to the total membership of a large group because in it several themes are existing at the same time. Much thinking, for example, may go on between the meetings of a professional association, and in the meetings themselves there may be considerable chaos and individual pairing, so that it is difficult for anyone to elucidate one common theme. It may be that several consultants or executives are needed to pick up different themes that are going on simultaneously. Furthermore, it is my observation that things that are causing concern in an organization may be concealed and are to be elicited only in small group meetings or by direct contact with individuals.

Much work needs to be done on the "vicarious" way an individual uses others to express his or her participation in several of the ongoing themes.

IMPLICATIONS FOR THE PATIENT

We and many of our patients and clients participate in large groups. How are we affected by them?

Robert was a senior executive in a large international corporation, which, while powerful, was under pressure from current changes in societal values. It was a corporation from whose management group I had, fortuitously, treated a patient some years before. I already had a picture, therefore, of both the organizational structure of the company and of the physical surroundings in which Robert worked. He, with his fellow senior executives, had the top floor of their building to themselves and reported directly, one on one, to the President.

Robert had been brought up in a family where his father, with his mother's silent collusion, physically threatened him frequently, and repeatedly told him that his actions and even his thoughts were inappropriate.

Robert complained of chronic depression. He defended against his various anxieties and his depression with a long-standing deliberate identification with the Nazis. Often in the evening he would walk in the city wearing a leather coat and secretly carrying a knife. Publicly he was very assertive, and he was aggressive in his corporate life.

Robert had been married for twenty-two years to a woman with whom he repeated the masochistic relationship he had with his parents. In private his wife denigrated him. She undercut his attempts to improve the marriage and she cast doubts on his professional ability. He retreated periodically to his place in the country, not only to peace and tranquility but also to an island of safety where he could pull himself together, away from his wife, his children, and his organization.

He formed a liaison with an attractive young woman in his own department. His peers in the executive group knew what was going on and, indeed, they seemed to enjoy it vicariously for themselves. They would ask him how things were between them, and would even send the pair together to meetings elsewhere around the country. Robert's activities seemed to act as an antidepressant for some of the rest of the group.

Robert also played the role of "hatchet man" in his company. One of his job functions was a violent one: to destroy, certainly psychologically, unwanted, scapegoated members of the executive group. In this capacity he had become something of a mythical figure. He was referred to by the name of "killer." When Robert had inflicted hurt on someone, the unfortunate executive left and the others felt much better.

In Robert's analysis we worked on his fear of senior executives, his castration anxiety, his fears of personal annihilation.

Much time also was spent in trying to determine which of the bizarre fantasies in Robert's life were properly his own and to what extent he acted out the phantasies of others. He came to a growing realization that his father and mother were psychotic in their thinking and functioned only marginally in their community. His wife, he concluded, was fighting off a recurrent intense depression and, in doing so, needed to depress him. Later in his analysis, they separated. He realized that his liaison with the woman at work was being aided and abetted, consciously and presumably unconsciously, by his colleagues in the company. When he ended the affair and changed the relationship to a working, task-oriented one, she entered into a similar sexual relationship with another member of the executive group. Robert was bemused to observe the same phenomenon: the group wondered what the two were doing, joked about them, and sent the new pair off together.

As his personal analysis progressed, Robert realized that he was performing violent roles on behalf of others who were asserting themselves vicariously, aggressively, through him. They thus enabled themselves to maintain their own apparent sense of decency and innocence. Robert's aggressive—sexual and corporate—behavior may well have been an antidepressant for the others as well as for himself. Since, too, he was successful at it, he aroused both fear and envy in his colleagues. When he abandoned these roles many of his peers went to considerable lengths to cast him back in them.

Interpretations to Robert in his individual psychoanalysis helped him see how he was being "used" in organizational meetings and, within his corporation, outside these meetings. We can see how his early childhood and his personal problems made him a "fit" for the executive group. He carried the projective identificatory parts of many of his colleagues. They seemed to want to hear about his sexual acting out and his aggression. They pushed him into violent behavior, possibly as a way of dealing with the depressive phantasies (unconscious) in the large group. He was behaving in this manner on behalf of the rest, as an antidepressant for them. When he stopped, he gained a personal sense of self: they became disturbed and depressed.

INTERPRETATION TO LARGE GROUPS

It is not clear in our clinical theories when to interpret to an individual this carrying out of certain roles on behalf of others and when not. Can we help a patient see when he or she should go back to his organizational meetings and, in turn, make interpretations, or try to turn subgroups into work groups? What is unquestionable, however, is that the interaction of group and personal psychodynamics have major effects on the lives of most of us, and knowledge of the one will increase our understanding of the other.

The elucidation of some of the psychodynamic patterns of large groups shows how the individual experiences alienation and isolation: how one becomes a member of a group, and may become de-skilled in it and thrown back into oneself to an isolated, internally chaotic state. Group meetings sometimes promote bizarre behavior and elaborate complex myths. Waves of discontent associated with these meetings move back and forth in the large group. Similarly, rumors move back and forth and mythologies grow in institutions, which are large groups separated by walls. The nature of leadership in large group meetings or in institutions or organizations needs further investigation. We need to understand these groups and interpret their effects upon individual patients in their personal therapies.

As we look at them and in a later chapter, at cultures and social systems, we see that individuals are often profoundly depressed by their membership in groups.

> The external boundary of the organization in which Robert worked was under enormous environmental pressures from the community. Many of its senior executives became depressed, and they projected this depression into various individuals in the organization, including into Robert. At times it was difficult for the analyst not to be depressed by Robert's depression. Because the analyst recognized the projective identification involved, however, he was less vulnerable personally, and he was also able to show to Robert that he was carrying the depression, as well as the violence, of the group.

CHALLENGING QUESTIONS

Many of our depressed patient who, in turn, depress us, are carrying depressive aspects projected into them by projective identification from the institutions or organizations in which they work. Much of the "acting out" by patients is a result of their being pushed by the group of which they are a part to do so to counter depression in the group.

We, too, are members of professional associations. How much of the chaos and depressive anxieties and phantasies present in all industrial and social organizations, including psychiatric and social science institutions (Menzies Lyth 1970), do we bear ourselves? I feel very strongly that often we fail to make interpretations about group processes when such interpretations would help individual patients or clients in individual psychotherapy or psychoanalysis. We avoid the known effect that participation in large groups and in crowds often leads to regressive processes. Many a resident or trainee has been told that that individual therapy may bring about considerable change in intrapsychic areas but less in personal relationships. By not looking at groups, and at the projective identificatory bits from them that our patients and ourselves bring to our consulting rooms, perhaps because we think that they are unimportant, do we, in almost exclusively focusing on individual therapy, unintentionally place limits on the therapeutic results?

Zalenik (1979), as we have seen, suggests that formal organizations aid—in fact coerce—individuals to suppress intrapsychic conflict, limit interpersonal conflict, and control expression of affect in order to concentrate energies and attention upon the purposes of the organization. He feels that a more effective application of psychoanalysis could begin with observations and theories of social science such as "Game Theory," "functional analysis," and "bureaucratic power relations." This view, however, is contradicted by observation of groups in which individuals or subgroups, particularly at the top of an organization, produce unanticipated, undesirable consequences at different levels in the group. We are brought back to the role of the individual, and of regressive forces, within organizations. Surely these regressions are more than merely "noise in the system" as Zalenik (1979) asserts. "One effect of coercion exerted upon individuals by organizations is to prevent regression and to establish a facade of hyper-normality" (p. 147). Here Zalenik, in apparent contradiction of his earlier assertion, admits that he is talking about a facade. If one studies social systems closely (Menzies Lyth 1970) it becomes apparent that this powerful organizational functioning *merely conceals* the regressive processes that are going on at an intrapsychic level in members of the group. There is greater difficulty in detecting the problems and anxieties in the organization if attention is focused on the "casualty" who carries or acts out these problems. Many depressed patients or clients in individual therapy may well be "casualties" designated to carry the depression and anxiety concealed in their organizations or institutions, anxiety about its value, its organizational functioning, or, indeed, anything else. In the same way, of course, some therapists may be the depressed "casualties," or targets of aggression, within their organizations.

SOCIAL SYSTEMS AS A DEFENSE

Jaques (1951, 1955) elaborates the idea that social structures come into existence not only to perform a task but to conceal or hold at bay the paranoid and depressive anxieties of their members. Jaques extends the concept of transference to include the relation of the individual to the social institution. He shows how individuals exploit the social institution to externalize their unconscious and, therefore, unidentified internal worlds.

Menzies Lyth (1970) develops these concepts. In her studies of a nursing service in a London teaching hospital she found that nursing practice was organized into specific tasks. One nurse, for example, would do all the bedpans, another the temperatures, and so on. Patients were referred to by numbers or diseases. "Good nursing" meant that the jobs were carried out, but the nurses were not involved with the patients as people. The nurses operated in this way to avoid close proximity with human beings who were in pain, were mutilated, or were dying. Menzies Lyth felt that had they been encouraged to face and work through the depressive anxieties endemic in the situation, these anxieties would have been modified and reduced. Instead they were denied both the personal satisfaction of personal contact with those they helped and the opportunity to develop mature ways of dealing with the unconscious anxieties and affects. Menzies Lyth believed that the method of coping was to adopt the primitive defenses of the institution. Mature students found this distressing and the better students left. Others carried on without apparent emotion or individual identity. The staff was idealized, presumably to defend against the patients' own anxiety about their illness or mortality.

Miller and Gwynne (1972) studied nursing homes for the severely handicapped. They discovered that, essentially, they were one of two types. Miller and Gwynne term these "the warehousing ideology model" and "the horticultural model." In the former the patients were treated as passive figures in "bins." Only their physical needs were met (though in the better examples of this type of home their physical needs were well met). When one resident of a "warehousing unit" protested by establishing a somewhat critical newsletter he was transferred to a mental hospital for bringing despair to what was described as "this happy home." "The horticultural model" embodies ideas about emotional and personal development that to many of us are appealing. Miller and Gwynne, therefore, were correspondingly horrified to discover that in many of these highly idealized homes, where fresh air and a new way of doing things were supposed to cure all, and magical hopes for severely handicapped people were displayed, some of the needs of the residents were neglected. Their basic needs for medicine and nursing care often were not being met, since all, patients and staff, were caught up in the ideology that medicine, and wheelchairs and crutches and the like, were unimportant details. Criticism of some examples of "the horticultural model" was equally badly received.

Therapists treat individuals from all kinds of social systems. They deal with individuals, or may themselves be such individuals, from groups whose social organizations or group defenses are not working, and depressive anxieties break out. A mature way to guard against vulnerability to the depressive anxiety is to recognize how the social system has been used by the individual, patient, or therapist, and to acknowledge these breaks in defenses. Such recognition and acknowledgement may lead to personal growth.

It seems, then, necessary to consider that the individual patient, client, and therapist participates in groups, and that he or she is subject to the subtle and covert psychodynamic forces of these organizations and social systems. Operating in many of them are regressive forces, a symptom of which is depression, which the individual denies, suppresses, represses, or avoids. Many of those who come for treatment by psychotherapy do so with depressive symptoms because they have failed at their work. As the therapist listens, his patient or client may put into him, by projective identification, his depressive symptoms and depressive coping mechanisms. These may well originate in the problems of the small or large group or the social system of which he or she is a part. It is easy to overlook this and focus exclusively upon the patient's early life or transference neurosis.

6

Cultural and
Social Factors

We have adopted various metaphors—"the Global Village," "the American Melting Pot," "the Canadian Mosaic"—to provide shorthand acknowledgement of the way individuals move from country to country, culture to culture, in numbers unprecedented in centuries before our own. A major theme of this book is that the therapist is a container for the projected conscious and unconscious affects, fantasies and phantasies of others. This makes therapists vulnerable to overload, to the rupturing of their sense of self, but it also provides them with a diagnostic tool. It is a tool that is especially useful when treating patients from different cultures, different social systems, and cultures that may use words differently and that sanction depressive symptoms in different forms.

Ali was a 40-year-old engineer from the Middle East who had come to North America to avail himself of the greater job opportunities in his field. He had been referred for consultation by his general practitioner because he suffered

145

repeated bouts of hypertension. It took Ali several weeks to bring himself to arrange the consultation. He could only come, he said, when he "felt it was acceptable" for him to do so.

When Ali discussed his hypertension he said that there was a family history: his father and his uncle had died of myocardial infarction. He denied that he himself had cardiovascular troubles, except that he had had a "coronary spasm" some ten years before. Careful probing elicited that this was not angina, chest pain, but that he, too, had had a myocardial infarction. Ali was a man who minimized his problems.

Ali talked about his work. Hesitantly he confessed to having difficulty with his partners. It seemed that he might have to leave the firm and find a job elsewhere. He was very reticent about all this.

The consultant found himself becoming quite depressed. He detected that the depressive feelings and fantasies within him were not his own, but Ali's, and this knowledge determined how the interview would proceed: he asked Ali if he were depressed. Reluctantly, because he was a proud man and he equated depression with weakness, but with some relief because he was understood, Ali confessed that he was. Indeed, he was profoundly depressed.

Ali had difficulty understanding the culture in which he found himself. He did not communicate well with his new professional colleagues. He grieved for his lost past. He doubted the wisdom of his decision to move, and he suffered a temporary rupture of the psychological boundaries that had previously maintained his sense of self. In his therapy work he talked about his difficulty in learning the new mores and the "language" of his new culture.

Ali came from a country where depression was considered a weakness that should be ignored. Ali, however, projected unconscious nonverbal phantasies, which evoked conscious feelings and fantasies in his therapist, and caused the therapist to feel depressed. The therapist recognized the source of his own depression and therefore could use his apprehension of Ali's unacknowledged feelings and make interpretations.

Through the communality of human experience we *can* understand depressed patients from various cultures. It is important to see, however, that patients may *express* this depression differently and how it may, in turn, affect ourselves.

> Harold, a 38-year-old consultant from West Africa, came into analysis because he had become impotent. He was concerned about the state of his marriage and his wife's apparent loss of sexual interest in him, and about his business, where several problems were exercising him. He began to worry about the state of his heart. He developed abdominal pains he thought might be indicative of an ulcer. He complained of multiple aches all over his body.
>
> Harold was a highly articulate man. He was widely read in English literature as well as versed in his own country's folklore, of which he was proud. He understood and used modern telecommunications, but from his tribal culture, he also believed in extrasensory perception, and that communication took place in magical ways. He was not in the least psychotic but carried a basic set of beliefs from one culture to another.
>
> Harold underwent a series of medical and surgical consultations and investigations because he firmly believed he possibly had several physical illnesses. As each test proved negative he was led to seek another. On his business trips to his former homeland he consulted the tribal healer about his various symptoms.
>
> As all this was happening, the analyst began to worry about various aspects of *his own* health. He wondered how he would manage to treat his patients if he became ill—he wondered about his analytic potency, that is. He had fantasies related to professional jealousy of the tribal healer in Africa.
>
> It became clear that Harold was experiencing a disguised depression. It took a form similar to hypochondriacal cases often seen in Western Europe and North America where hypo-

chondriasis is a reflection of a masked depression. Dealing with this in analysis had a most revealing effect. Harold's bodily symptoms, and his worries about them, disappeared, and he became what is, in North American terms, depressed. His analyst, having regained his therapeutic potency, also recovered from *his* body symptoms and was able to function in his role, working with this particular patient with an increased understanding of his background and respect for it.

This case illustrates not only that depressions may be disguised, but that there are major differences in the forms these guises take. Again the analyst was alerted to Harold's probable depression by the process of projective identification into the analyst, which aroused fantasies about personal illness and professional capability. The analyst was able to recognize from his own reaction that the patient actually had an underlying depression. The analyst then was able to interpret to Harold his depression about his potency, his marriage, and his work.

It is helpful to learn as much as possible about the symbols and metaphors from his or her childhood and background used by the patient, either from the patient or by familiarizing oneself with the other culture by reading and research.

SOCIAL CAUSES

A form of depression that also presents with bizarre physical symptoms was observed in Western Canada and was almost culturally specific (Heath and McKerracher 1959) to Ukrainian-Canadian women who lived on vast farmlands. The basic symptoms were hypochondriasis and crying episodes with depressive symptomatology, which seemed to worsen in the long Western Canadian winters.

Various therapeutic attempts were made. ECT was used and was at first successful. Drugs, antidepressants, were equally so, as were major and minor tranquilizers. All medical intervention seemed beneficial for a time, but as soon as the women were discharged from the hospital and returned to their small towns, their symptoms returned. This was very depressing to observe and constituted a major threat to the omnipotence of the hospital staff concerned. All biological and supportive psychotherapy methods seemed, at least immediately, effective, but upon the patients' returning to their communities the failure rate was almost total.

The women were quite depressed. They lived on very large and isolated farms. Their children were bused to schools that were miles away, for the whole day, even in the worst of weather. Their husbands were out in barns, repairing farm equipment and readying it for the summer. In any case, the husbands were enjoying a life they had chosen and one they found satisfying, and they usually met their peers quite frequently or worked with a hired hand. The wives were isolated socially, and for much of their time were physically alone. Because their culture did not permit it, they were unable to get in touch with the anger they felt about their husbands' and children's phantasied rejections of them. Their only recourse to a socially sanctioned form of handling their depression was to be admitted to the hospital for an "illness."

The hospital gave them much support. There were people there: doctors, nurses, ancilliary staff. They received a great deal of attention. The use of ECT and drugs seemed to give them sanction and respectability, confirming that they had a "medical complaint." There was a great deal of resentment when no drugs were given and an attempt was made, usually quite unsuccessfully, to show these patients and their partners and families that they were dealing with particular and difficult social–psychological situations.

The syndrome was a common psychiatric entity in the area and it was not easy for the therapists to admit that they were totally ineffective in dealing with this "social depressive illness." Nor was it easy for them to deal with their feelings of failure and vulnerability as psychiatrists. It was particularly difficult for some of the professional staff who were themselves of Ukrainian-Canadian background and had experienced the pattern when they were parented. There were few groups in these communities that could provide the women with a social network. As they rapidly became "casualties," but respectable ones with "illnesses," the idea of seeking social solutions did not seem to be readily acceptable or possible.

LANGUAGE DIFFERENCES

Depression is not a readily accepted cause for seeking help in many cultures, and the euphemisms to describe it change from place to place. An American therapist in England, or an English therapist in many parts of the United States, has to become aware of the different uses of words. In the United Kingdom the language varies between the Scots, the Northern English, and the Southern English.

"Northerners" especially, it seemed to me, did not find depression an easily accepted part of the cultural language. They would remark "I must get up and get on with things," or "I'm bothered." They voiced concerns about their "inability to cope." It became apparent that this was the language of depression in a culture where one, particularly if one were adult and male, could not openly admit to feeling depressed. If one heard a patient moralizing about his or her need to get on with things, one could assume that this was evidence of a struggle with depression, and that one should ask questions about sleep disturbances, recent object losses, and the like.

If one heard patients ask the therapist, on the other hand, "Can you cope?" one knew they were concerned about the therapist's ability to deal with patients' inner depression and symptomatology. Would the therapist, that is, be as easily depressed as they? Could their hidden angry or violent phantasies destroy the therapist, as they wished to destroy the ambivalently loved internal introjected object or internal parts of themselves?

In therapy with these patients, once one had identified the underlying depressive problem, it was possible to look at the psychodynamics of the neurotic depression or reactive depression, including the hidden anger at the real or imagined lost external object (represented by an ambivalently loved internal object).

SOCIOECONOMICS

Therapists treat patients from different socioeconomic as well as geographic backgrounds and these sets of mores and values differ considerably, even within the common North American culture. The young adult, often from the ghetto, who handles his depression by thieving may depress his therapist: the youth feels cheated and therefore steals. When the work proceeds and the thieving stops the youth may become severely depressed. The therapist then has a difficult therapeutic problem. If, on the other hand, the youth acts out by leaving treatment, the therapist, because his work has not succeeded, in turn feels cheated and he, too, may feel depressed on that account.

The wealthy patient who does not have to work presents problems of a different kind—the therapist has to guard against unfavorable self-comparisons and envy. The usual restraints and holding function of analyses and therapies do not work easily with such patients. One analyst who treated

movie stars told me that some of them were extremely difficult. When they became depressed they did not mind missing
sessions, much less paying for them. They would act out the
depression by running off to do a film on location, or have a
liaison in a far part of the world. This does not mean that the
wealthy cannot be analyzed, but that the form in which they
handle depressive anxieties and the symptoms may be different. They may act out aggression rather than regress into
dependency or angry depression within the therapy or analysis. Fortunately, much of this behavior responds to interpretation.

The *form* of depressive symptomatology and anxieties,
then, may vary between social classes or groups. Currently,
alcohol and drugs are the accepted antidepressants in some
groups; in some they are "acting-out" behavior, stealing, for
example. Some social groups handle their depression by organizational maneuvers, such as stock manipulation or attacks
upon other organizations. Violence through organizational
behavior may be a socially sanctioned antidepressant and
should be recognized as such.

SOCIAL MOBILITY

Patients (and therapists) may have moved socially, as well as
geographically.

Daniel, 35, was an extremely intelligent, educated, and
articulate professional who came from what is usually termed
a socially deprived background. He had been brought up in
the area of the city considered to be at the bottom of the social
scale. Daniel insisted, however, that it was not a slum. In his
analysis he remarked that many times in his childhood well-
intentioned social workers would come into his neighborhood
to find out why certain children were not in school. These
social workers, Daniel said, seemed to feel that the children in

hold

the community were deprived. They did not see that there was a great deal of social bonding and support. The unemployed fathers, for example, were at home all day, and they paid a great deal of parental attention to their sons and daughters—a benefit not enjoyed by the children in Daniel's present middle-class milieu, many of whose fathers were mostly absent in their sixty–seventy hour working weeks. Daniel's own father, in fact, was one of the few who had a job and Daniel, therefore, "suffered" from a lack of fathering, relative to his peers (although unlike many of them, he identified with a father who believed that work was important).

Daniel's parents and others were rankled by the community workers, who were unaware that they were out of step with their clients. Charitable organizations would bring in food baskets at Christmas and Thanksgiving and distribute them to families, often to those who did not need them. A rule of the community was to accept the food and trade and barter it. Since the donors felt good about what they were doing and the recipients redistributed the food there was no move on either side to change the process.

In his personal therapy Daniel was frustrated by the difficulty of having to describe from an adult middle-class ego state or self-state what it was like being a young child with a different ego state or self-state, the difficulty of a 35-year-old describing the experiences of a child. He complained that his analyst could not understand him because the analyst could not understand the background from which he had come. This, in fact, was an expression of Daniel's own difficulty in reconciling his current and childhood backgrounds. At other times Daniel felt that interpretations were unwanted donations. After a few months the analyst most probably had a fairly clear apprehension of Daniel's background and upbringing. It was necessary to show to Daniel that he had to deal with *his own* rejection of these in his current "middle-class" life.

Similarly, while the depression of many patients, like that of the women from the Canadian Prairies, may be an almost direct result of their social circumstances and it is important to understand the cultural background of all patients, the social evils to which some patients attribute their depressions, justly deserving of anger though these systems unquestionably may be, may be external embodiments of problems in their inner worlds.

Dorothy was a white, married academic; her husband, Philip, was black. They had made repeated unsuccessful attempts to have a child before Dorothy finally gave birth to a son.

Philip and Dorothy had left their country of origin, in part because of the professional opportunities elsewhere but also because, rightly or wrongly, they believed that mixed marriages were tolerated better in their new location.

Within Dorothy's analysis one had to deal with many fantasies about the child she had with Philip, and her fantasy that she had sinned by marrying a black against the wishes of her family. There was much material concerning her expectations for her son. These centered around the fact that he was of mixed race. In her analysis she worked through her depressive anxieties about his future in the world. Some of these anxieties were realistic ones about the probable restraints he would experience in his later life: restraints her husband experienced because of his color, as did other children of mixed marriages she knew.

When she had worked through these depressive anxieties, Dorothy began to talk of her hopes for her son. He would perform an important role in the United States, and he would help to unite blacks and whites. Through the analyst's mind flashed the dream of every American child: that he or she could become President of the United States. The analyst found himself looking, without any conscious reason, at his appointment book. He realized that the patient was talking about this theme on February 22nd, Washington's Birthday (Presidents' Day). The analyst interpreted to the patient that she wished her son to be President of the United States, the first of mixed race, who would thereby provide unity and a solution to some of the turmoil that had been going on. This interpretation was accepted.

Dorothy's pride in her son was linked to the personal pride in her ability to have had a child, which had overcome former feelings of inferiority she had felt about herself as a woman. Early childhood links to feelings of ineptitude and failure should not be minimized, but it was shown that her apparent omnipotent fantasies and depressive anxieties were, in fact, culturally based. Concern about racial tensions and racial discrimination was a realistic, appropriate reaction. That she could be depressed by her previous infertility was also realistic, and the phantasies that she had unconsciously destroyed the other "babies inside her" had to be dealt with. These valid causes for sadness and anxiety, however, were interwoven with particular fantasies of racial violence in societies, and these were related to her own violent phantasies.

Dorothy depressed her husband by her own depressive symptomatology. She had the phantasy that her marriage— "different races cannot get along together"—and her analysis, in the transference—"how can a therapist from another country understand me?"—were doomed to failure. For his part, her husband depressed Dorothy by his stories of the ghetto. As she recounted these stories to her analyst, in a deeply depressed way, he and she almost relived Philip's experiences in the slums where he had spent most of his early years.

The analyst and patient began to see the back-and-forth effect within the marriage, where one partner put depression in the other and the other passed it back in a cumulative way until both were almost overwhelmed.

Where we come from is a part of what we are. Our social organizations may make us vulnerable to one disorder or another. Our culture may determine the symptoms by which the disorder manifests itself. Our belief systems determine the way we describe it. If we leave one social system for a less familiar one we may leave many of our defenses against anxiety. It is important, therefore, that the therapist learn as much about the culture of the patient as he or she can.

The communality of human experience, however, makes it indeed possible for a therapist from one culture to understand a patient from another. The patient who says, "You do not understand me because you are of the wrong race" or "the wrong sex" or "the wrong country" or "the wrong class," is often wrestling with his or her internal problem of understanding himself or herself.

7

Summing Up

The classification of depression is fraught with difficulty. While newer types of classification that shift to more descriptive or operational definitions help to clarify the categorizing of symptoms, they do little to address the problems of differentiating cause. The interested reader might consult reviews by Kendell (1976) and Farmer and McGuffin (1989). The latter suggest that while there is still a differentiation between reactive and endogenous depressions and extensive clinical use of such a differentiation, there is no basis for continuing this traditional dichotomy. In my view this is arguable. Farmer and McGuffin, however, remind us that classifications of depression are merely working hypotheses. They also imply that many patients previously diagnosed as schizophrenic will be liable to reclassification under a category of affective disorder. Their statements, if carried to a conclusion, have profound unacknowledged implications, particularly for the clinical treatment of the various depressive disorders.

A search for chromosomal abnormalities and the genetics of depression continues. Some depressions seem to have a biological basis. Hitherto it has been emphasized that the treatment of bipolar depression, or endogenous depression be by physical methods. With the blurring of the boundaries between the so-called reactive/neurotic depressions and endogenous depressions, however, definitive modes of treatment have been eliminated. We are reaching the point when the clinical method of treatment used depends on the severity of the depression. This has major clinical and medical–legal implications.

Further confusion arises when patients present with depressionlike symptoms who may be suffering from disorders other than depression. Notable among these disorders is the schizoid sense of futility, whose symptoms are similar to those of a chronic depression. The schizoid sense of futility, however, results from a fundamental fault in early mother–infant relationships. The sufferers feel unable to relate to an external object and have the phantasy that they will devour such an object or will themselves be devoured. This leads to withdrawal, outwardly and inwardly. It is a basic fault in development that many people have. Physical treatments may be tried, but they are ineffective. Long-term psychotherapy or psychoanalysis is the treatment of choice.

Another category of patient is that of those who have suffered major assaults upon their sense of self and regress into a profound state of what seems to be depression. While the symptomatology is similar to depression, the major affect is shame. The two affects are not alike. The sense of failure in a major life goal may lead to a rupture in the sense of self. Repeated blows to a fragile sense of self result in symptoms that may be confused with recurrent depressions. Many individuals suffer these. In these kinds of cases the clinical condition is not depression.

Those who are prone to masochism have a tendency to

self-depreciation or self-effacement, which may give a clinical picture, again, similar to depression. Careful examination shows it to be an aspect of a masochistic character.

Those who suffer from a sense of guilt about an act for which they, consciously or unconsciously, feel responsible may suffer a depression. We feel guilty and depressed when we have transgressed against our internal moral codes: accidentally harming another (even in unconscious phantasy) results in depressive symptomatology, often lasting for days. It is easy to regard such a clinical picture as a depressive reaction. Similarly, if one has lost a relative whom one has ambivalently loved, and toward whom one has had, conscious or unconscious, death wishes, there may be the magical thought that one's unconscious phantasies have had their effect and the person's death is the result. The correct clinical diagnosis of the resultant state would be not merely grief or depression but guilty depression. It is the sense of guilt that may immobilize the particular individual for a long period of time.

These other categories of apparent depression are often hidden in current prevalence studies, showing up as false-positives. They may represent some of the 30 percent whom antidepressant medications fail.

In my own residency in psychiatry, in a particular program where drugs were not used, the treatment even of cases of endogenous or of psychotic depressions, which would now be called "major depression," by psychotherapy of an interpretive and supportive kind seemed to be as effective as results I have seen when current biological methods were used. Nevertheless, particularly in the United States, those who are diagnosed as having a severe depression and do not receive treatment by biological methods may consider that they have not had sufficient treatment since, for example, drugs have not been given. They may resort to malpractice suits. There do not seem to be any current legal implications in cases where patients have been treated by biological methods when long-term forms of psychotherapy possibly could have been considered.

In a similar, somewhat critical vein, self psychology may have its disadvantages as well as its advantages. With the looking at ruptures between the environment and a patient, evaluation of the rupture by the therapist and the patient provides a replacement object (external) that might resonate with internal needs (repairing internal objects) for particular patients. This process may inhibit that of allowing the patient to regress so that more fundamental flaws in character structure, arising from problems very early in the patient's life, may be examined. Many therapists find it difficult to tolerate the very regressed conditions found in those who suffer from basic ego weakness (Guntrip 1960) or those with a borderline personality who regress by acting-out.

THE TRANSFERENCE/
COUNTERTRANSFERENCE

Some of the studies have been summarized in Chapter 3. From these we see a movement to broaden the concepts of transference and countertransference, which has been of great clinical and theoretical benefit. An important development is the recognition of the constant to and fro between patient and therapist in all sessions and in the minds of both between sessions—outside the sessions, that is. Therapists and patients become internal objects in each other's lives. Within the sessions themselves there is a transfer of feelings between patient and therapist. Fantasies (conscious) and phantasies (unconscious) are projected into the therapist as well as vice versa. All this necessitates a view of ego psychology and ego functioning that allows a reconceptualization of the ego as it functions as a cognitive organ. Put into the therapist or analyst are *all* of the different psychic parts of the patient. Many of them are the patient's feelings associated with fantasies and phantasies. They are put into the therapist or analyst (in both a verbal and nonverbal way) by projective identification. The understanding by the therapist of his or her counterreaction to the patient may be diagnostically useful in processing the patient's projections, and in the formulation of subsequent interpretations.

That the therapist helps "by listening and being there" has a psychodynamic explanation: therapists project into their patients and clients, consciously and unconsciously, by projective identification, hopes, expectations, and, unintentionally, directions. Using an extended view of the transference/countertransference paradigm, we can see that simply by his or her presence, the therapist can in a nonverbal way transform what the patient says and reflect it back, either immediately or later, or give some nonverbal response that will change the patient's projections. These are then reflected back in a more healthy way.

The major part of therapeutic work is still by verbal interpretation. The concept that one can use what is projected into one as a basis for interpretation, however, is one of great practical value to the therapist. Consciously or unconsciously, the therapist discerns the patient's projections and makes an interpretation to the patient, unconsciously processing the projections at the same time.

The foregoing is an extension of Bion's concept of the container and the contained. According to Bion, the baby projects raw elements (beta-elements) into the mother, who, by her reverie, turns these into more coherent elements for the child to introject. Bion thus explains how the holding and facilitating environment conceptualized by Winnicott (1965) actually may work.

Within the therapist's ego, part of which is conflict-free, is another unconscious part, which is receptive to the projections for evaluation by the conflict-free part of the ego, a receiver for such projections. This does not mean that it is an open system between patient and therapist. There is a boundary, a "person boundary," between them. The relationship is not a merger, nor is it a symbiotic one.

The recent psychoanalytic literature contains few studies of counterreactions to the patient that consider *how* the therapist is made to feel by the patient, what the therapist's fantasies about the patient are, and how these might be used to learn what is happening within the patient and the transference. There are notable exceptions in the psychoanalytic literature (for example, Khan 1964, McDougall 1985). I have tried to do so.

THERAPISTS' FAILURES

Depressed patients may cause their therapists to become depressed. The depressed therapist then, in turn, may depress the patient even further. This ping-pong effect is a danger in therapy. It may be produced in a nonverbal way.

It is necessary also to recognize that the therapist may have other than straightforward depressions aroused in him or her. It can be frustrating to deal with the chronically masochistic patient, for example. If there is little therapeutic movement the therapist may be depressed about his or her professional capabilities. The failure with this type of patient, however, may be a subtle one. While the masochistic patient cannot consciously move the therapist to fulfil his or her object-relation requirements to fail, some therapists, suffering from a sense of guilt and depression over their supposed inadequacy, become aggressive. In so doing they play the sadistic role in a sadomasochistic process for the patient.

It is often difficult to admit we fail as therapists, and that a therapy should be terminated. Continuing ineffective therapy, however, is masochistic in itself, and is a coping mechanism. The purpose of such therapy is to ease the therapist's depression, which is based on guilt over failing.

I once thought it was helpful to hear that at worst, as analysts and therapists, all we can do is simply fail. Further reflection leads me to believe that dealing with a patient who may be masochistically failing in order to fulfill a requirement of his or her masochism is not a simple matter. It is difficult for any therapist to terminate therapy or to transfer patients who, apparently, are hopeless. These failures threaten our sense of self, our narcissism, and our considerable feelings about our work. To fail, then, is not so easy. It is something that arouses many feelings, especially depression over failure, in us. Yet to continue because we have been caught in the masochistic depressive symptomatology of a patient who is only too willing to make us a partner in his or her masochism, to play out needed object relationship roles, is a therapeutic failure. Sometimes there is no way out of this impasse. While it is a threat to our omnipotence and omniscience to fail, sometimes we do.

A therapist may sometimes (unconsciously) select a particular patient to fail with. All the therapist's need for failure is then "packaged" into one patient so that he or she, as a therapist, may go on to succeed with others. As some patients have a masochistic need to fail, they may take on this role and fulfill the therapist's unconscious purposes. Understanding the concept of projective identification is thus of enormous value. Failure with the patient we see at four o'clock, say, or with the one we do not like very much, can be averted if we realize what we are doing. Recognition of the process by the therapist means that it does not have to happen. Failure is not inevitable. The therapist's need to fail can be guarded against; the patient's need to collude in failure can be overcome by the therapist in the therapeutic work.

Similarly some patients may need to fail with a particular

therapist. They may need to fail with one therapist and not with a later one—and this could lead to despair in the former, who may feel personally responsible, guilty, and so on, and to a sense of triumph or omnipotence in the latter, if the process is not recognized. The success of the second therapist, however, may not be due to therapeutic means that are not available to the first. It may be that the patient has put his or her failure into the first therapist and, by a splitting mechanism, can then have a "good" therapy or analysis with the later one. This means that some problems, splitting mechanisms, for example, have to be dealt with in the later therapy. Does "splitting" happen in other areas of the patient's life? Does he or she need to fail with the first spouse and not with the second? Or scapegoat one of the children and scapegrace another? Or idealize or denigrate different members of the group with whom he or she works?

This phenomenon of "splitting" explains how individuals, patients and therapists included, may be casualties, being victimized or lionized in the societies, organizations, or institutions to which they belong.

LEARNING ABOUT BOUNDARIES

Between two people there is a transmission of affects, fantasies (conscious), and phantasies (unconscious) in a reciprocal way. With training, foresight, insight, and skill, therapists can use what crosses the interpersonal boundaries between their patients or clients and themselves to help these patients gain insight into what is happening between them in the here and now, and by extension, what happens between themselves and others in their everyday lives. The depressed patient, for example, can come to realize how he or she depresses others and, conversely, how others (individuals or groups or organizations) depress him or her.

Because therapists are attuned to their patients, in such sessions they are vulnerable to the patients' depression. Empathic identification is required in order to project one's psychic part into the patient and then take it back, to get a "feel" for the patient, and to really "listen" to the patient and understand the feelings and fantasies of what it is like to be within him or her. The boundary between ourselves and our patients is like a semipermeable membrane—between one psyche and the other. The unconscious of the patient is in touch with the unconscious of the analyst or therapist, and vice versa.

The boundaries are protective of the therapist, and so is the recognition that the patient is constantly projecting into the therapist's ego (part of which is conscious, part unconscious), which is a container for the patient's projections. If the therapist maintains the boundary function on a cognitive basis, he or she need not be overwhelmed by the patient's projective identifications. The patient's depressive symptomatology, therefore, can be understood and *felt* by both the patient *and* the therapist, but the therapist is not overwhelmed. The therapist can come to learn to *"feel* depressed" temporarily, but not *"be* depressed" by the patient. Boundary function or malfunction occurs on an intrapsychic basis in the patient at both the ego level, consciously and unconsciously, and in other parts of the psyche. Intrusion of superego functions into the patient's ego, for example, can be overwhelming at times (as well as what is termed in classical theory an overwhelming by the id or drives)—in other terms, using the concept of the internal world, of conflicts between internal objects or object relationships. These are conflicts that also may be projected into the therapist: a superego criticism in the patient, for example, that is experienced in both patient and therapist.

Patients, in turn, can learn about boundary functioning and maintenance. They may also have to be protected by boundaries from a therapist's depression, which may have come from his or her outside sources. Therapists also use projective identification, and patients also are attuned in sessions and in a regressed receptive mood. The therapist needs personal insight about his or her internal world to minimize the risk of affecting the patient in an untoward way.

AGAINST OPENNESS

Discussing the "countertransference" with the patient has inherent dangers. Once done, the therapy has shifted into an "encounter" mode of therapy and interpersonal boundary function has decreased. If patients cannot understand the effect they have on others this will repeat itself in the transference, consciously and unconsciously, unintentionally, spontaneously, where it can be observed, analyzed, and interpreted. When many therapists get involved on a routine basis in telling how they feel about a patient—or in telling when they are in a particular personal-life or family crisis—the roles are being reversed: patients are being used for therapists.

There may be occasions when it is reasonable to tell a patient the effect that he or she has upon the therapist. In my experience, it is useful when there is excessive patient acting out that is affecting others in adjoining office areas or in the patient's life. Patients, at times, by virtue of their own psychodynamics and psychopathology, deny the violent effects they have upon others. They project, by projective identification, their own internal unconscious need to exert control into the therapist, who has to recognise this. The therapist might suggest to the patient that he or she needs to get self-control, and that certain ego functions, which may be conflict free, have been put into the therapist for safekeeping because the patient is unconsciously afraid of his or her own violence, violence that he or she fears might destroy the "goodness" and functioning parts of the ego within him- or herself.

While I have been perturbed about the moralistic approach in the training of candidates for psychotherapy, there are obviously some restrictions on therapists' behavior that have to be taught and imposed. Sexual behavior with patients is forbidden. Therapists indulge in this in some cases as an antidepressant to their own personal-life problems. Self-recognition by the therapist should inhibit such behavior. The skilled therapist is attuned to his or her intrapsychic workings. This lessens the internal boundary between the unconscious and the conscious and permits self-analysis. It allows fantasies to emerge into the therapist's ego as aids to therapy.

ORGANIZATIONAL AND GROUP DIFFICULTIES

While most patients are members of groups, at work in businesses, factories, institutions, and institutes, how they are affected by the depressions over work failure or interpersonal difficulties or whatever that arise in such groups has been a hitherto neglected area of study. How patients become depressed, how therapists become depressed, and how the former affect the latter (or vice versa) has been elaborated in these chapters.

It may be remembered that the diagnosis of the depressed patient, particularly in an outpatient–inpatient unit, is often made by a committee. Such a committee is a group involved in small-group psychodynamics. A group, as we have seen, can become depressed. The depressing lives of people can be depressing to the case conference or clinical team. This, if unrecognized, will in turn affect the diagnosis and treatment of the patient.

When we move to study the psychodynamics of the large group we are observing the workings of institutions of which many of us are part. Many mental health institutes and clinics are not always very easy places in which to work. Many staff members may be depressed on an ongoing basis by what is happening in them. They then have to treat patients suffering

from depression. The patients' narratives remind them of
these problems and issues in the organization. Sometimes a
ping-pong effect ensues; one depressed person affects another. We also need to recognize that social institutions elaborate complex behaviors to conceal depressive and paranoid
anxieties for their members.

It is easy for a therapist to handle his or her anxiety or
depression about a patient by overasserting authority; sometimes, if the therapist is a physician, by prescribing drugs or
physical methods of treatment such as ECT. The physician is
then caught in what might be a circular argument. Drugs are
prescribed, particularly antidepressants, if there is a possibility
that the patient has a biological component in his or her
"illness." Thereafter in the patient's life, the fact that he or she
has received drugs is suggestive that the patient has, if not a
history of biological illness, at least a predisposing factor to
such illness.

It is possible that a therapist may be so depressed by what
is going on in his or her personal life that this affects the
individual consultation and psychotherapy process with the
patient. I agree with the view that all therapists should have
personal therapy or, ideally, psychoanalysis. Throughout this
book I have stressed the crucial need for therapists to examine,
by self-scrutiny or by consultation with their peers, how they
are affected by their patients and by their own living and
working environments.

CRITICIZING "WOUNDED HEALERS"

At a psychological level all therapists are regarded as threatening. For some it may be necessary to handle their anxiety
about people who may understand the unconscious of the
human mind by ridiculing them or by focusing on their
defects, hence the popularity of articles about "wounded
healers." The acceptance that there are unconscious processes
makes people anxious, because these processes are beyond

conscious control. By attacking therapists in a social situation, an individual is able to distance him- or herself from the work the therapist does with patients and from his or her own internal psychological world.

This is not to say that all therapists, at all times, are entirely healthy. People with extreme psychological difficulties should not be admitted to psychiatric, psychological, or mental health training programs. Overcompensation for the concern that harmful candidates not be admitted (a further difficulty is getting an unsuitable candidate to leave a training program, even when such a student causes turmoil within the program itself) has resulted, however, in some training programs selecting orderly, obsessive-compulsive, noncreative individuals who, in turn, may be seriously hampered as therapists however culturally acceptable their psychopathology may be. It should be recognized that *moderately* troubled individuals can function extremely well as therapists and may function particularly well with certain types of psychopathology in their patients. One has only to think of the remarkable work of Harry Stack Sullivan, for example.

It should also be recognized that the work of the average-functioning therapist will be frequently disrupted by depressed patients. As therapists are attuned and open to patients and to the human unconscious, they may be particularly vulnerable to human problems, including depression of all forms, from all sources within their patients.

CULTURAL VARIATIONS

Patients vary in their language and their culture. While there is sufficient communality of human experience to enable most therapists to treat most patients, plainly, some therapists work better with some patients than with others, and the converse is also true. Some women feel more comfortable with a female therapist. Sometimes this is because they believe a woman can better understand a woman; sometimes it is to avoid dealing with problems with men. Generally speaking, in my view, the relatively normal, well-trained psychiatrist, psychoanalyst, or psychotherapist can deal with *most* of the wide range of clinical problems presented to him or her. Insightful therapists, on the other hand, will not choose to treat patients or clients who do not make "psychological fits" with them as a therapist.

As societies have become more interdependent, movement and communication between one culture and another have become swift. How do changes, and mechanical and informational explosions, in their external worlds affect the internal worlds of individuals? In order to cope, some try to become more self-controlled. In my experience, this mechanism rarely works.

Therapists treat many patients who suffer from an existential depression over what they feel they are as humans in a rapidly changing, complex world. Therapists, too, have to deal with their own experience of the patient's world and not be overwhelmed by it. In all of us, however, is a human core of warmth and understanding that meets the internal conflicts in our identifications with parts of the mechanical world around us. Patients cannot be treated by machines. Even if a computer could be so programmed, the internalization of the computer would only add in the internal world of the patient a still greater sense of mechanization, which would cause more disruptions within the mind. The therapeutic experience of a live person, feelings and all, catching the back-and-forth projections and introjections is a necessary component of effective therapy. This also necessitates that the therapist, who is attuned to the patient, be equally attuned to him- or herself: that he or she recognizes the effects of the introjections of projective identification from the patient. Vulnerable therapists protect themselves by understanding. In so doing, they and their patients learn to deal with the real human beings they both are.

Bibliography

Abend, S. M. (1989). Countertransference and psychoanalytic technique. *Psychoanalytic Quarterly* 43:374–395.

Anzieu, D. (1984). *The Group and the Unconscious.* London: Routledge & Kegan Paul.

Arlow, J. A. (1985). Some technical problems of countertransference. *Psychoanalytic Quarterly* 56:164–174.

Bacal, H. A., and Newman, K. M. (1990). *Theories of Object Relations: Bridges to Self Psychology.* New York: Columbia University Press.

Balint, M. (1957). *The Doctor, the Patient and His Illness.* New York: International Universities Press.

Bebbington, P. E., Brugha, T., MacCarthy, B., et al. (1988). The Camberwell Collaborative Depression Study 1. Depressive probands: adversity and the form of depression. *British Journal of Psychiatry* 152:754–765.

Bion, W. R. (1961). *Experiences in Groups.* London: Tavistock.

_____ (1962). *Learning from Experience.* London: William Heinemann, Ltd.

Blos, P. (1980). The life cycle as indicated by the nature of the transference in the psychoanalysis of adolescents. *International Journal of Psycho-Analysis* 61:145–152.

Blum, H. P. (1983). The position and value of extratransference interpretation. *Journal of the American Psychoanalytic Association* 31:587–618.

Buckman, J. (1985). Self-destructive behaviors. In *Depressive States and Their Treatment,* ed. V. Volkan, pp. 221–236. New York: Jason Aronson.

Calder, K. T. (1979). Psychoanalytic knowledge of group processes, panel, chairperson B. E. Moore. *Journal of the American Psychoanalytic Association* 27:145–156.

Chediak, C. (1979). Counterreactions and countertransference. *International Journal of Psycho-Analysis* 60:117–130.

Cooper, A. M. (1987). Changes in psychoanalytic ideas: transference interpretation. *Journal of the American Psychoanalytic Association* 35:77–98.

Eastwood, M. R., and Kramer, P. M. (1981). Epidemiology and depression (editorial). *Psychological Medicine* 2:229–234.

Eysenck, H. J. (1965). The effects of psychotherapy. *International Journal of Psychiatry* 1:99–144.

Ezriel, H. (1957). The role of transference in psychoanalytic and other approaches to group treatment. *Acta Psychotherapeutica* 7:101–116.

Fairbairn, W. R. (1952). *Psychoanalytic Studies of the Personality.* London: Tavistock.

Farmer, A., and McGuffin, P. (1989). The classification of depression: contemporary confusion revisited. *British Journal of Psychiatry* 155:437–443.

Ferenczi, S. (1919). On the technique of psycho-analysis. In *Further Contributions to Psycho-Analysis,* pp. 177–189. London: Hogarth Press, 1926.

Freud, S. (1905). Fragment of an analysis of a case of hysteria. *Standard Edition* 7:3–125. London: Hogarth Press, 1953.

———— (1910). Future prospects of psychoanalysis. *Standard Edition* 11:139–152. London: Hogarth Press, 1957.

———— (1915). Observations on transference love. *Standard Edition* 12:157–171. London: Hogarth Press, 1958.

———— (1917a). Mourning and melancholia. *Standard Edition* 14:237–258. London: Hogarth Press, 1957.

———— (1917b). Analytic therapy. *Standard Edition* 16:243–464. London: Hogarth Press, 1963.

———— (1920). A case of homosexuality in a woman. *Standard Edition* 18:145–175. London: Hogarth Press, 1955.

———— (1921). Group psychology and the analysis of the ego. *Standard Edition* 18:67–144. London: Hogarth Press, 1955.

———— (1940). An outline of psychoanalysis. *Standard Edition* 23:141–208. London: Hogarth Press, 1964.

Gitelson, M. (1952). The emotional position of the analyst in the psychoanalytic situation. *International Journal of Psycho-Analysis* 33:1–10.

Guntrip, H. (1960). Ego-weakness and the hard core of the problem of psychotherapy. *British Journal of Medical Psychology* 33:163–184.

_____ (1961). *Personality Structure and Human Interaction.* London: Hogarth Press.

_____ (1968). *Schizoid Phenomena, Object Relations and the Self.* New York: International Universities Press.

Hartmann, H., Kris, E., and Lowenstein, R. (1946). Comments on the function of psychic structure. *Psychoanalytic Study of the Child* 2:11–38. New York: International Universities Press.

Heath, S. (1971). Group psychodynamics and the psychiatric case conference. *Canadian Psychiatric Association Journal* 16:223–226.

Heath, S., and McKerracher, D. G. (1959). Impressions of a common psychiatric entity. *Canadian Medical Association Journal* 80:896–897.

Heimann, P. (1959). Counter-Transference. *British Journal of Medical Psychology* 33:9–15.

Jacobs, T. J. (1973). Posture, gesture and movement in the analyst: cues to interpretation and countertransference. *Journal of the American Psychoanalytic Association* 21:77–92.

Jaffe, D. S. (1986). Empathy, counteridentification, countertransference: a review with some perspective on the "analytic instrument." *Psychoanalytic Quarterly* 55:215–243.

Jaques, E. (1951). *The Changing Culture of a Factory.* London: Routledge & Kegan Paul.

_____ (1955). Social systems as a defence against persecutory and depressive anxiety. In *New Directions in Psycho-Analysis,* ed. M. Klein, P. Heimann, and R. E. Moncy-Kyrle, pp. 478–498. New York: Basic Books.

Kendall, R. E. (1976). The classification of depression: a river of contemporary confusion. *British Journal of Psychiatry* 153:15–28.

Kernberg, O. (1965). Notes on the countertransference. *Journal of the American Psychoanalytic Association* 13:38–56.

_____ (1989). The temptations of conventionality. *International Review of Psycho-Analysis* 16:191–206.

Khan, M. M. R. (1964). Ego-distortion, cumulative trauma and the role of reconstruction in the analytic situation. In *The Primacy of the Self,* pp. 59–68. New York: International Universities Press.

King, P. (1980). The life cycle as indicated by the nature of the transference in the psychoanalysis of the middle-aged and the elderly. *International Journal of Psycho-Analysis* 61:153–160.

Klein, M. (1952). Notes on some schizoid mechanisms. In *Developments in Psycho-Analysis,* pp. 292–320. London: Hogarth Press.

Kreeger, L., ed. (1975). *The Large Group: Dynamics and Therapy.* London: Constable.

Laplanche, J., and Pontalis, J-B. (1973). *The Language of Psychoanalysis.* New York: Norton.

Little, M. (1951). Counter-transference and the patient's response to it. *International Journal of Psycho-Analysis* 32:32–40.

Maeder, T. (1989). Wounded healers. *The Atlantic* 263:37–47.

Mahler, M. (1968). *On Human Symbiosis and the Vicissitudes of Individuation.* New York: International Universities Press.

Main, T. (1975). Some psychodynamics of large groups. In *The Large Group,* ed. L. Kreeger, pp. 57–86. London: Constable.

Malcolm, J. (1985). *In the Freud Archives.* New York: Vintage Books.

McDougall, J. (1985). *Theaters of the Mind: Illusion and Truth on the Psycho-analytic Stage.* New York: Basic Books.

McGuffin, P., and Katz, R. (1989). The genetics of depression and manic depressive disorder. *British Journal of Psychiatry* 155:294–304.

McLaughlin, J. T. (1987). The play of transference: some reflections on enactment in the psychoanalytic situation. *Journal of the American Psychoanalytic Association* 35:557–582.

Meltzer, D. (1981). The Kleinian expansion of Freud's metapsychology. *International Journal of Psycho-Analysis* 62:177–186.

Menzies Lyth, I. (1970). The functioning of social systems as a defence against anxiety. In *Containing Anxiety in Institutions: Selected Essays.* London: Free Association Books, 1988.

Miller, E. J., and Gwynne, G. V. (1972). *A Life Apart.* London: Tavistock.

Mumby, T. (1975). Large groups in industry. In *The Large Group,* ed. L. Kreeger, pp. 272–290. London: Constable.

Murphy, J. M. (1990). Depression in the community: findings from the Stirling County Study. *Canadian Journal of Psychiatry* 35:390–396.

Olinick, S. L. (1980). *The Psychotherapeutic Instrument.* New York: Jason Aronson.

Persad, E. (1989). Major depression. *Medicine in North America* 36:6542–6545.

Phillips, K. A., Gunderson, J. G., Hirschfeld, R. M. A., et al. (1990). A review of the depressive personality. *American Journal of Psychiatry* 147:830–837.

Pick, I. B. (1985). Working through the counter-transference. *International Journal of Psycho-Analysis* 66:157–166.

Poland, W. S. (1984). On the analyst's neutrality. *Journal of the American Psychoanalytic Association* 32:245–268.

Racker, H. (1948). The counter-transference neurosis. *International Journal of Psycho-Analysis* 34:313–324.

Rathling, D. L., and Chused, J. F. (1988). Transference across gender lines.

Journal of the American Psychoanalytic Association 36:77–104.

Rioch, M. J. (1970). The work of Wilfred Bion on groups. *Psychiatry* 33:56–65.

Rorsman, B., Grasbeck, A., Hagnell, O., et al. (1990). A prospective study of first-incidence depression—the Lundby Study, 1957–1972. *British Journal of Psychiatry* 156:336–342.

Rosenbaum, M., and Richman, J. (1970). Suicide: the role of hostility and death wishes from the family and significant others. *American Journal of Psychiatry* 126:1652–1655.

Rosenfeld, H. (1965). *Psychotic States.* New York: International Universities Press.

Sandler, J. (1983). Reflections on some relations between psychoanalytic concept and psychoanalytic practice. *International Journal of Psycho-Analysis* 64:1–11.

Searles, H. F. (1965). *Collected Papers on Schizophrenia and Related Subjects.* New York: International Universities Press.

Segal, H. (1973). *Introduction to the Work of Melanie Klein.* London: Hogarth Press.

—— (1977). Psychoanalytic dialogue: Kleinian theory today. *Journal of the American Psychoanalytic Association* 25:363–370.

Silverman, M. A. (1985). Countertransference and the myth of the perfectly analysed analyst. *Psychoanalytic Quarterly* 54:175–199.

Stengel, E. (1964). *Suicide and Attempted Suicide.* Baltimore: Penguin.

Thorner, H. A. (1981). Notes on the desire for knowledge. In *Do I Dare to Disturb the Universe? A Memorial to Wilfred R. Bion,* ed. J. S. Grotstein, pp. 589–599. Beverly Hills, CA: Caesura.

Turquet, P. M. (1974). Leadership—the individual and the group. In *Analysis of Groups,* ed. G. S. Gibbard, J. J. Hartmann, and R. D. Mann, pp. 349–371. San Francisco: Jossey-Bass.

—— (1975). Threats to identity in the large group. In *The Large Group: Dynamics and Therapy,* ed. L. Kreeger, pp. 87–144. London: Constable.

Volkan, V., ed. (1985). *Depressive States and Their Treatment.* New York: Jason Aronson.

Waksman, J. D. (1986). The countertransference of the child analyst. *International Review of Psycho-Analysis* 13:405–416.

Winnicott, D. W. (1965). *The Maturation Process and the Facilitating Environment.* New York: International Universities Press.

Wisdom, J. O. (1987). Bion's place in the troika. *International Review of Psycho-Analysis* 14:541–552.

Index